# Enchanting Woodland BIRDHOUSES

LUCINDA CLAIRE MACY

**NORTH LIGHT BOOKS**
CINCINNATI, OHIO
www.artistsnetwork.com

## A Note About Safety

To prevent accidents, keep safety in mind while you work. Use the safety guards installed on power equipment; they are for your protection. When working on power equipment, keep fingers away from saw blades, wear safety goggles to prevent injuries from flying wood chips and sawdust, wear headphones to protect your hearing, and consider installing a dust vacuum to reduce the amount of airborne sawdust in your woodshop. Don't wear loose clothing, such as neckties or shirts with loose sleeves, or jewelry, such as rings, necklaces or bracelets, when working on power equipment. Tie back long hair to prevent it from getting caught in your equipment. People who are sensitive to certain chemicals should check the chemical content of any product before using it. The author and editor who compiled this book have tried to make the contents as accurate and correct as possible. Plans, illustrations, photographs and text have been carefully checked. All instructions should be carefully read, studied and understood before beginning construction. Due to the variability of local conditions, construction materials, skill levels, etc., neither the author nor North Light Books assumes any responsibility for any accidents, injuries, damages or other losses incurred resulting from the material presented in this book.

### Metric Conversion Chart

| TO CONVERT | TO | MULTIPLY BY |
| --- | --- | --- |
| Inches | Centimeters | 2.54 |
| Centimeters | Inches | 0.4 |
| Feet | Centimeters | 30.5 |
| Centimeters | Feet | 0.03 |
| Yards | Meters | 0.9 |
| Meters | Yards | 1.1 |
| Sq. Inches | Sq. Centimeters | 6.45 |
| Sq. Centimeters | Sq. Inches | 0.16 |
| Sq. Feet | Sq. Meters | 0.09 |
| Sq. Meters | Sq. Feet | 10.8 |
| Sq. Yards | Sq. Meters | 0.8 |
| Sq. Meters | Sq. Yards | 1.2 |
| Pounds | Kilograms | 0.45 |
| Kilograms | Pounds | 2.2 |
| Ounces | Grams | 28.4 |
| Grams | Ounces | 0.04 |

Enchanting Woodland Birdhouses. © 2002 by Lucinda Claire Macy. Manufactured in China. All rights reserved. No part of this book may be reproduced in any form or by any electronic or mechanical means including information storage and retrieval systems without permission in writing from the publisher, except by a reviewer, who may quote brief passages in a review. Published by North Light Books, an imprint of F&W Publications, Inc., 1507 Dana Avenue, Cincinnati, Ohio 45207. (800) 289-0963. First edition.

Other fine North Light Books are available from your local bookstore or art supply store or direct from the publisher.

05 04  03  02  01    5  4  3  2  1

Library of Congress Cataloging-in-Publication Data

Macy, Lucinda Claire
    Enchanting woodland birdhouses / by Lucinda Claire Macy.
        p. cm.
    ISBN 1-58180-071-1
    1. Birdhouses--Design and construction. I. Title.

QL676.5 .M3325 2002
690'.8927--dc21                                                          2001045227

Editor: Maggie Moschell
Designer: Stephanie Strang
Production editor: Jane Friedman
Production coordinator: John Peavler
Production artist: Cheryl VanDeMotter
Photographers: Lucinda Claire Macy and Al Parrish
Drawings by: Lucinda Claire Macy

# About the Author

As far back as I can remember, I have had a love affair with Nature. Growing up in a rural setting fostered this strong relationship with the flora and fauna of the forests and hills. I was also encouraged to express and develop my creative and artistic impulses at an early age. I was impassioned about violets, forget-me-nots, ferns and frogs! I painted and drew them on paper; I loved wood and woodworking. As years were added, so were skills in printmaking, pottery, stained glass, woodworking, as well as architectural rendering and graphic arts. The great love for small things in the woods also grew to encompass all aspects of the natural world, landscape and architecture. The desire to capture and communicate the beauty and wonder of these things to others has remained a great force behind my pursuits to this day. I have always greeted challenges with the spirit of creativity and have raised three children using these skills. I now live in the mountains of northeastern California with my pets, projects and gardens. And what could be better!

*Visit Lucinda at* **www.elucinda.com**

## Dedication

I dedicate this book to my loving parents who showed me the wonders of Nature and encouraged my art, thereby making this book and all the things that I have accomplished possible. I also dedicate this book to all people everywhere who have that desire to "make and do" and are receptive to my encouragement and enthusiasm for the creative process.

## Acknowledgments

First of all I would like to thank my daughter Jane for being my patient and good model for many hours under hot lights while Mom tried to figure out just what it was she was doing! I would also like to thank my son Noah for using his literary skills to help me sort out all the writing—the readers will greatly benefit from this! I would also like to thank my other daughter, Arindelle for her loving encouragement to get through this project that indeed brought many new challenges. I would extend a heartfelt thank you to my wonderful editor, Maggie—for patience, understanding, encouragement and vision. And also, to David Lewis for being the first one to see the possibilities of making a book and approaching me with the idea. *Thank you all.*

# TABLE OF CONTENTS

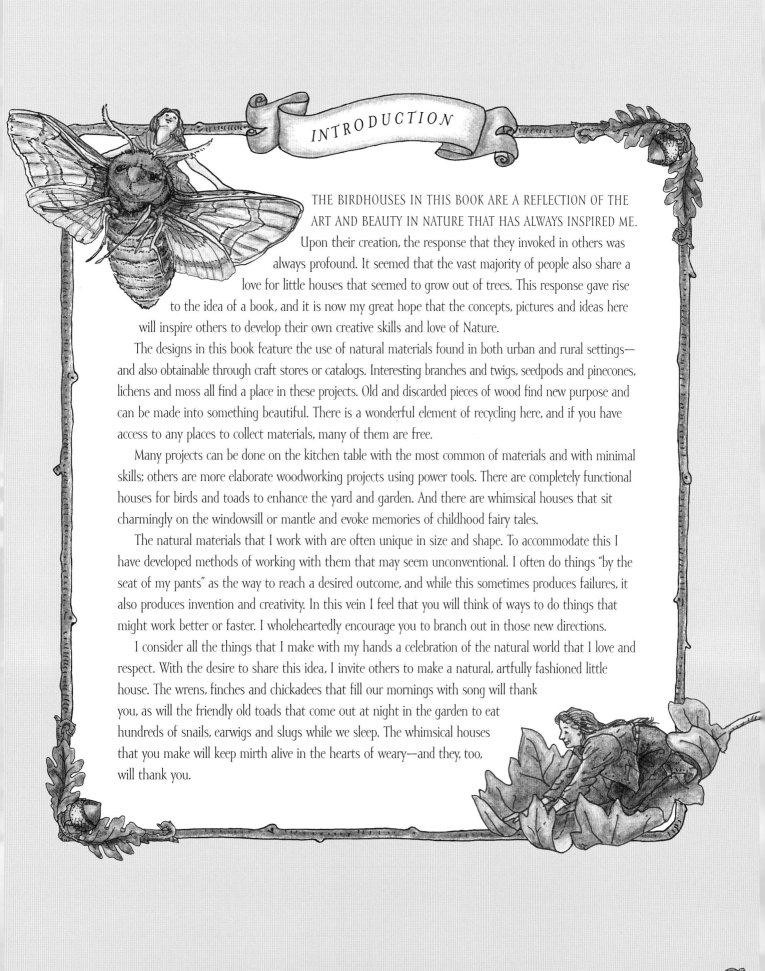

THE BIRDHOUSES IN THIS BOOK ARE A REFLECTION OF THE ART AND BEAUTY IN NATURE THAT HAS ALWAYS INSPIRED ME. Upon their creation, the response that they invoked in others was always profound. It seemed that the vast majority of people also share a love for little houses that seemed to grow out of trees. This response gave rise to the idea of a book, and it is now my great hope that the concepts, pictures and ideas here will inspire others to develop their own creative skills and love of Nature.

The designs in this book feature the use of natural materials found in both urban and rural settings—and also obtainable through craft stores or catalogs. Interesting branches and twigs, seedpods and pinecones, lichens and moss all find a place in these projects. Old and discarded pieces of wood find new purpose and can be made into something beautiful. There is a wonderful element of recycling here, and if you have access to any places to collect materials, many of them are free.

Many projects can be done on the kitchen table with the most common of materials and with minimal skills; others are more elaborate woodworking projects using power tools. There are completely functional houses for birds and toads to enhance the yard and garden. And there are whimsical houses that sit charmingly on the windowsill or mantle and evoke memories of childhood fairy tales.

The natural materials that I work with are often unique in size and shape. To accommodate this I have developed methods of working with them that may seem unconventional. I often do things "by the seat of my pants" as the way to reach a desired outcome, and while this sometimes produces failures, it also produces invention and creativity. In this vein I feel that you will think of ways to do things that might work better or faster. I wholeheartedly encourage you to branch out in those new directions.

I consider all the things that I make with my hands a celebration of the natural world that I love and respect. With the desire to share this idea, I invite others to make a natural, artfully fashioned little house. The wrens, finches and chickadees that fill our mornings with song will thank you, as will the friendly old toads that come out at night in the garden to eat hundreds of snails, earwigs and slugs while we sleep. The whimsical houses that you make will keep mirth alive in the hearts of weary—and they, too, will thank you.

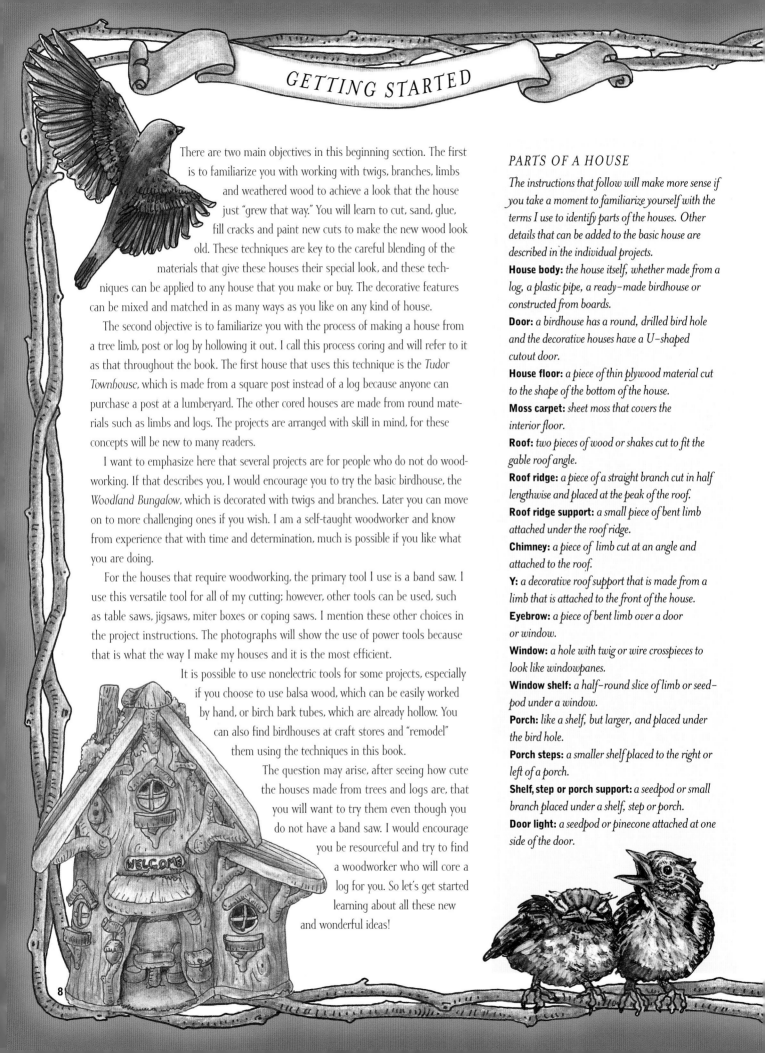

There are two main objectives in this beginning section. The first is to familiarize you with working with twigs, branches, limbs and weathered wood to achieve a look that the house just "grew that way." You will learn to cut, sand, glue, fill cracks and paint new cuts to make the new wood look old. These techniques are key to the careful blending of the materials that give these houses their special look, and these techniques can be applied to any house that you make or buy. The decorative features can be mixed and matched in as many ways as you like on any kind of house.

The second objective is to familiarize you with the process of making a house from a tree limb, post or log by hollowing it out. I call this process coring and will refer to it as that throughout the book. The first house that uses this technique is the *Tudor Townhouse*, which is made from a square post instead of a log because anyone can purchase a post at a lumberyard. The other cored houses are made from round materials such as limbs and logs. The projects are arranged with skill in mind, for these concepts will be new to many readers.

I want to emphasize here that several projects are for people who do not do woodworking. If that describes you, I would encourage you to try the basic birdhouse, the *Woodland Bungalow*, which is decorated with twigs and branches. Later you can move on to more challenging ones if you wish. I am a self-taught woodworker and know from experience that with time and determination, much is possible if you like what you are doing.

For the houses that require woodworking, the primary tool I use is a band saw. I use this versatile tool for all of my cutting; however, other tools can be used, such as table saws, jigsaws, miter boxes or coping saws. I mention these other choices in the project instructions. The photographs will show the use of power tools because that is what the way I make my houses and it is the most efficient.

It is possible to use nonelectric tools for some projects, especially if you choose to use balsa wood, which can be easily worked by hand, or birch bark tubes, which are already hollow. You can also find birdhouses at craft stores and "remodel" them using the techniques in this book.

The question may arise, after seeing how cute the houses made from trees and logs are, that you will want to try them even though you do not have a band saw. I would encourage you be resourceful and try to find a woodworker who will core a log for you. So let's get started learning about all these new and wonderful ideas!

## PARTS OF A HOUSE

*The instructions that follow will make more sense if you take a moment to familiarize yourself with the terms I use to identify parts of the houses. Other details that can be added to the basic house are described in the individual projects.*

**House body:** *the house itself, whether made from a log, a plastic pipe, a ready-made birdhouse or constructed from boards.*

**Door:** *a birdhouse has a round, drilled bird hole and the decorative houses have a U-shaped cutout door.*

**House floor:** *a piece of thin plywood material cut to the shape of the bottom of the house.*

**Moss carpet:** *sheet moss that covers the interior floor.*

**Roof:** *two pieces of wood or shakes cut to fit the gable roof angle.*

**Roof ridge:** *a piece of a straight branch cut in half lengthwise and placed at the peak of the roof.*

**Roof ridge support:** *a small piece of bent limb attached under the roof ridge.*

**Chimney:** *a piece of limb cut at an angle and attached to the roof.*

**Y:** *a decorative roof support that is made from a limb that is attached to the front of the house.*

**Eyebrow:** *a piece of bent limb over a door or window.*

**Window:** *a hole with twig or wire crosspieces to look like windowpanes.*

**Window shelf:** *a half-round slice of limb or seedpod under a window.*

**Porch:** *like a shelf, but larger, and placed under the bird hole.*

**Porch steps:** *a smaller shelf placed to the right or left of a porch.*

**Shelf, step or porch support:** *a seedpod or small branch placed under a shelf, step or porch.*

**Door light:** *a seedpod or pinecone attached at one side of the door.*

WELCOME

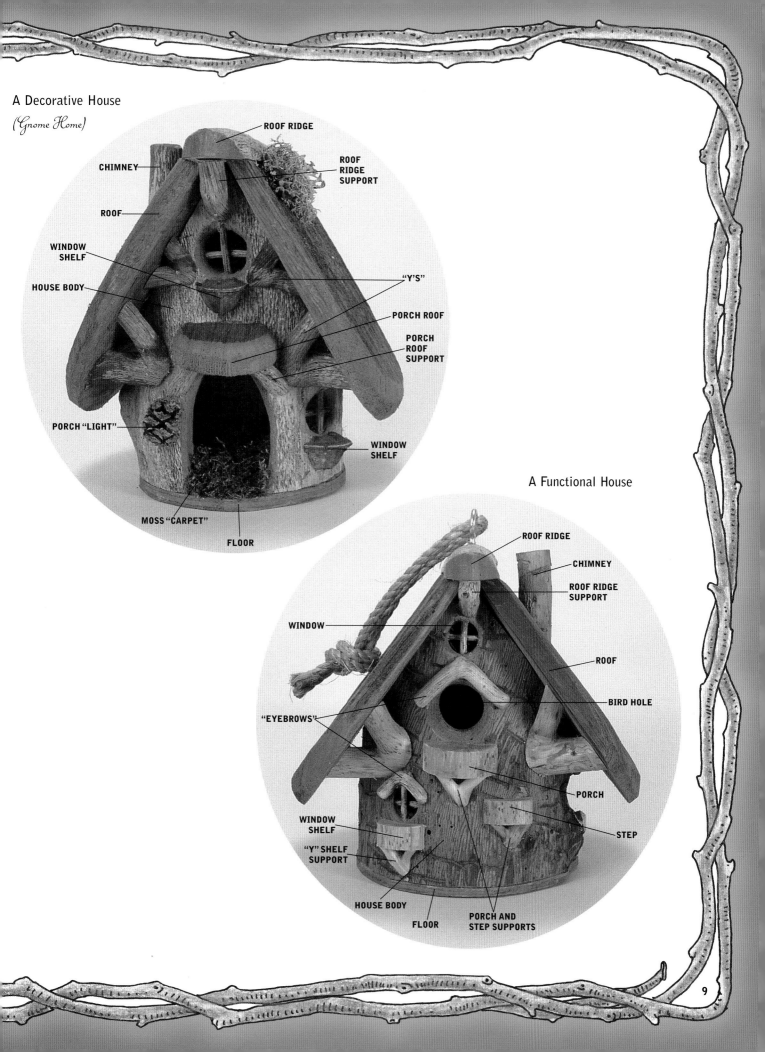

A Decorative House
*(Gnome Home)*

ROOF RIDGE

CHIMNEY

ROOF RIDGE SUPPORT

ROOF

WINDOW SHELF

HOUSE BODY

"Y'S"

PORCH ROOF

PORCH ROOF SUPPORT

PORCH "LIGHT"

WINDOW SHELF

A Functional House

MOSS "CARPET"

FLOOR

ROOF RIDGE

CHIMNEY

ROOF RIDGE SUPPORT

WINDOW

ROOF

BIRD HOLE

"EYEBROWS"

PORCH

WINDOW SHELF

STEP

"Y" SHELF SUPPORT

HOUSE BODY

FLOOR

PORCH AND STEP SUPPORTS

*Outside my shop, I have a collection of limbs, logs and shakes used for making houses.*

Materials

Most of the materials used for the houses are free if you have time to search for them. Once you start looking, you will develop an eye for the kind of things you want. I search for limbs that look as if they are "waltzing," meaning they have interesting curves, bends and twists. Typically, they are the dead limbs that have been pruned from trees or blown down by winter storms. All of these limbs can be used—from the twigs at the tip to the larger part at the base, and everything in between. The limbs that work the best have loose bark that is easily removed or no bark at all.

If you do not live in a wooded area, you might try contacting landscaping companies or anyone who trims trees on public or private property. Usually the dead trees and limbs are chipped or cut up on location, but these workers may be more than happy to let you haul away some choice branches and logs.

Although a walk in the woods is an enjoyable way to collect materials for houses, I did not have to walk very far to get the logs I use for most of my house bodies—they were "rescued" from the firewood pile. I've also purchased round cedar fence posts from a home-and-garden store that can be cut and used for several house bodies. For smaller houses, consider using birch bark tubes that come in a variety of sizes and are already hollow. Driftwood is twisted and would add character to any house, but wood that has sand in it will dull your saw blades.

Look for wood that is dry (not "green") and free from cracks (although thin cracks can be filled with sawdust and glue). The logs should be fairly straight because the saw blade is vertical and won't be able to cut the core from a crooked log without cutting through the side

**It is very important** *to consider the source of the materials you will be gathering to make your houses. Most people who love and respect Nature also are aware of the fragility of our natural environment. Care needs to be taken not to cut or disturb dead trees that are the habitat of birds or other wild creatures. I look for limbs that are already on the ground around the base of large, older trees. Branches from orchard trees that must be pruned each year are a wonderful source of wood that would otherwise be thrown away. I think that common sense dictates that you should make sure that it's OK to remove materials from the places where you hunt. I encourage you to gather natural materials in a responsible and respectful manner and enjoy doing it!*

*In my shop I keep baskets of moss, seedpods and the small twigs that I use in the windows. Having a variety of materials close at hand makes working more efficient and pleasant.*

*These are good limbs to collect because they have nice curves and bends and can be used as the Eyebrows, roof supports and chimneys for the houses. Limbs without bark or with loose bark will save you the trouble of re-moving it.*

*Here are three typical logs for house bodies. Notice that the bark is removed; if you leave the bark on the log, it will eventually come off and take your decorations with it (with a few exceptions as I will mention later). The wood for the house bodies can range from 3" to 7" (7.5cm to 18cm) in diameter and 6" to 10" (15cm to 25.5cm) tall. Each project specifies the best log size to use.*

of the house. Soft woods are the easiest to work with, especially for beginning woodworkers. These include cottonwood, ash, aspen, birch, cedar and pine (although the pitch in pine will coat saw blades and sanders). The first four are my favorites. Oak and applewood can also be used, but these harder woods are more challenging to work with and will dull your tools more quickly. Look for logs that have unique features such as interesting grain, small knots and natural holes that you might work into the designs. Occasionally you might find a hollow log. The last project in the book is for this stroke of good fortune.

You will also want to keep a sharp eye out for seedpods and other small decorations. Acorns, eucalyptus seedpods, and redwood pine cones are used for door lights, window shelves and other accents. The best time to collect them is in the fall or early winter. Also look for moss, which is used for "carpet" and for roof decoration.

Another recycled material that I often use is old cedar or redwood shakes from house roofs that are discarded when new ones are put on. These make the best roofs for all kinds of houses. New ones will work if you can't find old ones. The old ones have a nice, weathered look, but the new ones will fade with time or you can put a gray stain on them to make them look older. Old fence boards or barn wood are other good roof materials; new fence boards will weather in one season outdoors.

Once you have the idea of looking for limbs and branches for creating houses, you will begin to see them everywhere, and I guarantee that a walk around the block or through the woods will never be the same!

*These weathered shakes are my favorite material to use for roofs. The small round gravel is used for the River Rock House and can also be used for stone foundations on other houses. If you don't have a creek for gathering gravel, you can purchase some at a garden center or craft store.*

# Tools

This list of tools includes the power tools that are used for the projects, but please keep in mind that you do not need all of them for all the projects. There are alternatives to power tools, and some projects such as the River Rock Tower do not require any tools.

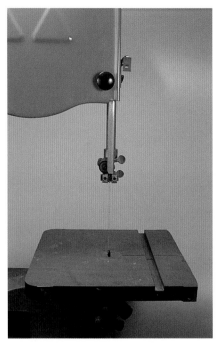

*This is my Delta band saw that I use for all my cutting. This larger saw enables me to core out taller houses. A smaller band saw will work fine for small houses.*

- **Band saw:** I use a 14" (35.6cm) Delta band saw with a riser block added to the neck to extend the cutting height a few inches. Any band saw that is in good working condition and is adjustable will work for making these projects. The cutting height and depth of the saw determines how tall the house can be, but you can make the smaller houses such as the Woodland Fairy House or Woodland Gnome Home with just about any band saw. You can cut all the decorative limbs and seedpods on any band saw.

- **Blades:** There are a variety of band saw blades on the market that will work. To core a log for the house bodies, I have found that a $\frac{1}{4}$" (6.4mm) blade with 4 teeth per inch (tpi) that has a flexback is best. A blade with 6 tpi can be used, but it will be slower.

- **Table saw:** Even though I make all my cuts with a band saw, most people would use a table saw for any of the projects using dimensional lumber (flat boards) and so I am listing it as a tool.

- **Scroll saw or jigsaw (table model):** These saws are an alternative tool for many of the things that I do with a band saw. I want to mention them since many woodworkers own them.

- **Brad gun and compressor:** Your brad gun should be able to use brads from $\frac{3}{4}$" to 1" (2cm to 2.5cm) long. Using a brad gun will save a lot of time. For years I nailed my houses together with small brads, which took a long time. Often I had to drill pilot holes for the brads. A friend lent me a small brad gun and now I wonder how I ever survived without it.

- **Electric drills:** You can use either a handheld drill or a drill press. The drill press is always straight and more controllable. A steady hand with a handheld drill will also work fine.

- **Cordless drill:** I use a cordless drill for drilling pilot holes and inserting screws into the roofs and floors. You can also use an electric drill for making the pilot holes and a screw driver for inserting the screws.

- **Spade drill bits:** I call these "paddle bits" and I use a variety of sizes, from $\frac{3}{4}$" to $1\frac{3}{8}$" (2cm to 3.5cm), for window holes and door holes.

- **Belt sander (table model):** I have found this tool saves much time and labor over just using a sanding block for smoothing the wood.

- **Hot glue gun:** This is handy for securing decorations such as twigs and seedpods before you nail them. However, I want to stress that this type of glue does not hold up for outdoor use.

## Smaller tools and materials for house building (from left to right)

- **Needle nose pliers**
- **Diagonal pliers** for cutting small twigs, wire and nails
- A tiny **drill bit** for drilling holes for screws
- A large **rubber band** that I use in place of clamps for gluing because they work especially well on curved surfaces
- Two **spade bits**, or paddle bits
- A large **wood rasp** for rounding the edges of the larger holes and roof edges
- A smaller **round rasp** for rounding the edges of windows and doors
- A **hammer**
- A **punch** for countersinking nails
- **Garden clippers** or small pruning shears for cutting branches that are finger size or smaller
- Large **pliers** for removing bark
- A **sanding block** with a metal 80-grit surface

Not pictured:
- **Wood screws** that are sold in bulk at hardware stores in 1" and 1¾" (2.5cm and 4.5cm) sizes. They are also called Sheetrock, drywall, or speed screws.

## Other tools and materials (starting on the left)

- A **cordless drill** used for putting in screws and for pre-drilling holes. I have two of them so that I do not have to change bits as often
- **Screws** that are from 1" to 1½" (2.5cm to 3.8cm) long
- A **glue gun** that I often use to hold something in place before I nail or screw it down
- A tube of **Liquid Nails** construction adhesive for exterior use. I use this glue for attaching a roof or a roof ridge or for mounting a house on a post.
- A small **brad gun** that uses brads from ⅝" to 1" (1.6cm to 2.5cm)
- Titebond solvent-based **construction adhesive** used for attaching rocks as in the River Rock Tower project
- Elmer's Squeez'n Caulk, a latex and silicone **caulking glue** that is great for filling cracks because it does not run
- Titebond II **wood glue** for exterior use

There are many glues on the market and new ones coming out all the time. I try as many as possible. You may have ones that you like already. If the house you're making is for outdoor use, you will want the materials, including the glue, to be waterproof. I always add screws and nails to outdoor houses so they will be sturdy enough to endure the elements.

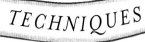

 Painting

The three bottles on the left are a copper patina kit that is used on the River Rock Tower roof (see page 14), and can be used on any metal house parts.

Acrylic paints are used to make any fresh cuts look old. I use them to paint the house floors, the window and bird holes, and other finishing touches. I mix Territorial Beige with a little Wedgewood Blue to tone it down slightly. Straight gray paint never looks quite right because weathered wood is really a shade of brown. I use a mixture of Golden Brown and Ivory when painting cedar or birch. When I fill a crack in the wood with glue and sawdust (see the next page), I often paint the patch to match the surrounding wood. Most people never see the repair.

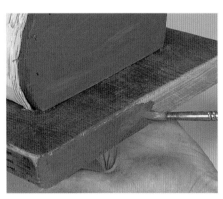

A fresh cut on old wood can be made to look more natural by painting it with arylic paint. Thin the paint with water to a milklike consistency so that it will soak into the wood and be transparent enough for the natural grain to show through.

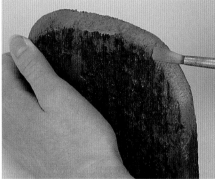

Paint the edges of the roofs and any other cut areas on the natural wood. This is the gray-brown paint I mix that seems to go with everything. It blends in well and gives a natural look. It's a good idea to paint all places where a new cut or sanding has been done. This makes the houses look completely natural, as if they grew that way.

## Filling Cracks

*Occasionally, you will find that pieces don't fit together and a gap is created or the wood cracks. These flaws are easily repaired with glue and sawdust. You can use this technique to fill gaps anywhere they happen, such as where an uneven floor is attached to the house body or a gap where the roof meets the house body. Since the gap shown in this photo is under the roof, it doesn't have to be waterproof; hot glue and sawdust can be used for these cosmetic repairs.*

*Hot glue is convenient for this patch because it sets up quickly and won't run into places you do not want it to go. To avoid burning yourself, pat the sawdust into the glue using a stick, not your fingers. This patch does not show from the front. The extra sawdust can be brushed off once the glue is set.*

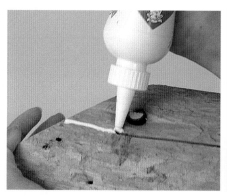

**1 Fill the crack with glue.**
To fill a crack in the back of an outdoor birdhouse, use a waterproof glue such as Elmer's Squeez'n Caulk, which is siliconized latex glue. First the glue is applied to the crack. Try to keep the glue confined to the crack because smeared glue is hard to remove from the wood surface. If the crack is quite deep and wide, fill it with a layer of hot glue before adding the waterproof glue and the sawdust.

**2 Add the sawdust.**
Sawdust that matches the wood is sprinkled over the glue. You will find that there are different colors and textures of sawdust in your work area. The sawdust that comes from the work table where you sand and rasp the house usually matches well for filling cracks. If your sawdust doesn't match well enough to hide the patch, you can paint the patch with a matching color acrylic paint when the glue is dry.

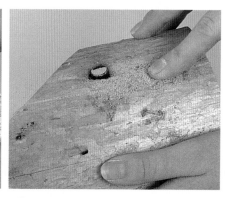

**3 Tamp the sawdust.**
Pat the sawdust into the glue with your fingers. The deeper the glue goes, the stronger the patch will be. Wipe off any excess glue while it is still wet by rubbing a bit of sawdust over the smeared glue until it forms a ball. You can lightly sand this area after the glue dries. If you sand too much, you will make a lighter-colored place on the weathered wood. The glue and sawdust mixture is very strong and will actually serve to strengthen the house.

## THE BASIC STEPS

1. *Design the house body*
2. *Cut the roof angles*
3. *Drill the windows and door holes*
4. *Core the house body*
5. *Cut the door*
6. *Reassemble the house body*
7. *Make the floor*
8. *Add the roof*
9. *Add the decorations*

These basic construction concepts and directions pertain to all the houses made from logs that are hollowed out or cored. The instructions for adding the decorations (Ys, eyebrows, etc.) can be used for all types of houses—log houses as well as ones made from dimensional lumber or ready-made birdhouses.

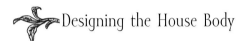 Designing the House Body

*First look at your log and try to see it as a house. Consider the grain, any interesting knots, spots where a limbs are attached, and if the log has a lean or a bend to it. A crack can be turned to the back and filled with glue and sawdust. Here are three logs of varying size, color and texture that would make delightful houses. Gnarled knots, wrinkles and prominent grain give a house more character than plain logs. I look for logs without bark so I don't have to remove it.*

*When drawing the house design on the log, try to use the knots and bumps in the design. Putting bulges on the sides and at the bottom allows you to work on the house from the front without it rolling around as would happen if the lump was on the back. Bulges or knots that are too high on the front can interfere with the placement of windows, doors and Ys. Also make sure the bottom is flat and the sides are vertical to ensure uniform walls when the log is cored.*

**If you are planning** *to make a functional birdhouse, it is important to know what makes a good, safe birdhouse. Birds are cavity dwellers who build their nests in something shaped like a hollow tree. Birdhouses shaped like a shoe box or a human house are not the right shape. Birds need a house that's tall and cylindrical so the nest can be built below the opening to protect the eggs from predators. The door has to be the right size and the right height above the floor (this distance varies with different species of birds). I feel that the reason my designs are so well used by the birds is that they resemble their natural homes. Each birdhouse in this book     lists the types of birds that it attracts.*

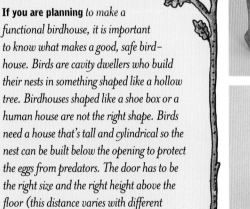

*Here are the three completed houses that show how the unique features of the logs can be incorporated into the house design. The houses on the right and left are gnome homes and the house in the center is a functional birdhouse.*

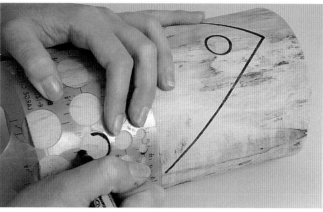

**2** **Draw circles for the windows and the door.**
Next add the circles for the window(s) and for the door if it's a bird-house. Each project will describe the distance from the door to the windows so you can get a sense of the correct proportions. Leave room for decorations, such as Eyebrows over the windows and seedpods for door lights. Allow a finger's width on all sides of a window hole or a door opening. Allow at least two fingers' width between a door opening and an upper window. These circles are ¾" to ⅞" (1.9cm to 2.2cm). Since you'll be drilling these holes, you don't have to draw perfect circles.

**1** **Draw the roof angle lines.**
First draw the lines for the roof angle. Mark the center of the top on the wood where you want the peak, then angle your line down to equal points on each side. The angle that I like is about 55°, which is steeper than the 45° that is typically used for a roof. I use a flexible plastic ruler to draw the line with a felt-tip pen.

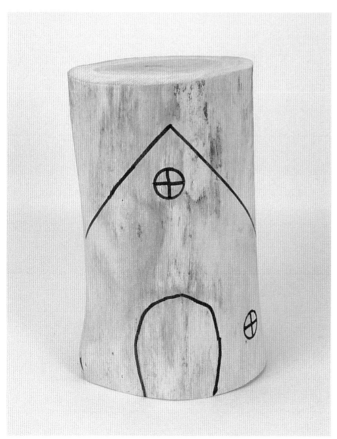

*Notice that the roof doesn't go all the way to the top of the log. I wanted to make the house look like a stout gnome home, so I didn't need to use the whole log. Try to envision the house you want, then adapt the length of the log accordingly.*

*The doors and upper windows should be centered on the log. The various parts should comfortably fit the size of the wood face. It is important not to crowd the features or to put window openings too close to the roof line or the door openings. Leave room for decorations that you will add later.*

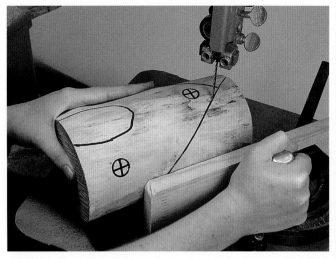

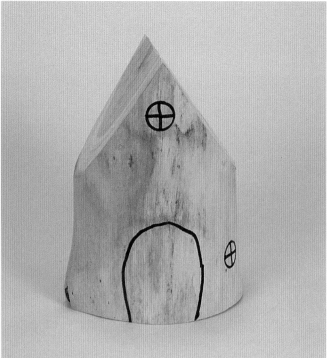

### 3 Cut the roof angles.

Use a band saw to cut the roof angles. (I recommend using a miter guide if you have not done a lot of cutting with a band saw.) Since the log is round and might roll, hold the wood securely. The saw blade must be sharp; I use a new blade for each new project because a dull blade is difficult to use and is always a safety hazard. If you don't want to use a band saw on a small house, you can cut the roof angles with a hand saw and a miter box.

If the cuts are a little rough, you can even them out after the house has been cored. You will be able to sand and rasp it more easily when the house is hollow.

*You should be well aware of the safety precautions for each power tool you use. Protective eyewear is important and you should never put your hands in the path of the blade. The precaution I would like to share pertains to your state of mind. You should never use power tools when you are feeling ill, sad or upset. Using power tools requires a clear, focused and assertive state of mind so that you have power over the power tool. Anything that causes preoccupation can result in a weak grip on the wood, and that's how accidents can occur. If you're not having a good day, do some work such as sanding and rasping with hand tools. You may find that this can be very relaxing.*

### 4 Drill the window holes.

To avoid cracking the wood, drill all window and door holes before you core the house. The holes are drilled with the spade drill bit specified in each project. This house is clamped in a portable workbench for stability. The holes must go straight in at least 1" (2.5cm) deep so that they will be deeper than the final thickness of the wall. Birdhouses have round doors; gnome and fairy house doors are U-shaped and are cut with a saw as shown in step 8.

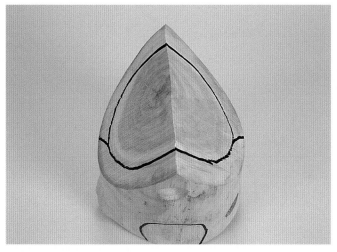

**5** **Draw the lines for coring.**
You will need a sharp blade and a log that sits flat and vertical on the saw bed. If the log is not vertical, the blade will cut through the wall and ruin the house body (and may cut your fingers). Once the log is cored and glued back together, you can cut the bottom at an angle if you want the house to have a tilt to it.

First draw the lines to follow when you core the log, which will cut the house in half. The wall thickness should be about 1" (2.5cm) for large houses such as birdhouses or toad houses, and ¾" (2cm) for fairy and gnome homes. Walls that are too thin make a weak house and are a cutting hazard.

**6** **Cut the front of the house on the band saw.**
The first cut enters from the side and cuts along the front of the house. Keep a firm grip on the log as you cut.

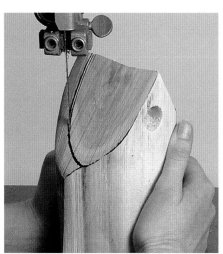

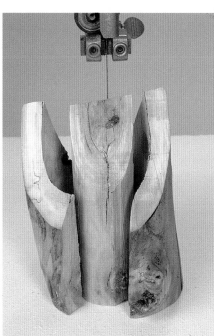

**7** **Make the second cut for the back of the house.**
The second cut follows the back line and hollows out the rest of the house.

**8** **Cut out the door.**
If you aren't making a birdhouse, you will need to cut out the door. Cutting the door is easier to do now because the body is hollowed out and cut in half. Use a band saw, jigsaw or coping saw for this step.

## Reassemble the Body

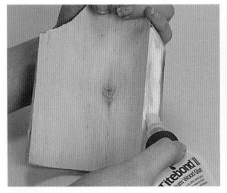

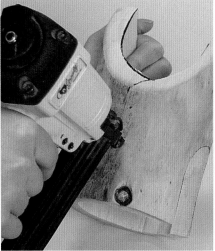

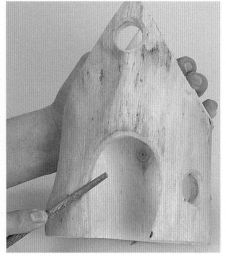

**9** **Glue the house together.**
Apply glue to each seam, put the halves together, and line up the edges as you press the halves together. Titebond II is a good glue for outdoor houses. Hot glue can be used for indoor houses, although I should warn you that it is difficult to make hot-glued parts fit tightly; if you don't work quickly, there will be a gap at the seam. If you're using a glue that has a drying time, clamp the house with rubber bands while the glue sets. If you don't have large rubber bands, use pieces of panty hose or elastic.

**10** **Nail the house together.**
It's best to wait until the glue is set before nailing the sides together, but if the house is clamped securely, you can go ahead and nail the sides together. Use a brad gun or a hammer and nails with small heads. Place the nails near the roof line so that the roof overhang will hide them. You want a nice, tight bond for the two halves.

**11** **Smooth the edges.**
Rasp the edges of the door and window holes to remove the sharp corners. You could also use a rolled piece of coarse sandpaper.

## Making the Floor

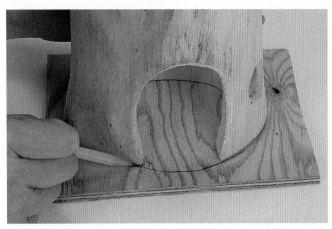

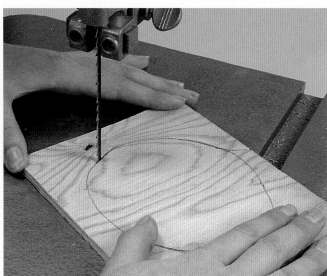

**12** **Trace the floor.**
To make a floor, trace the footprint of the house onto a piece of ¼" (6.4mm) plywood. Mark the location of the door to help line up the floor when you glue it to the house body. Draw past the door opening on the natural curve or add a slight bulge. Moss will be glued to the floor and the slight protrusion is more welcoming, like a doormat.

**13** **Cut out the floor.**
Cut out the floor with a band saw, jigsaw or coping saw.

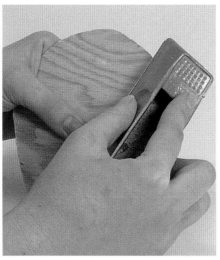

**14 Sand the edges.**
Smooth the edges of the floor with your sanding block or sandpaper to remove splinters. Round the bottom edge slightly. If you are making a functional birdhouse, don't glue or nail the floor to the house. Skip to step 17 and paint the floor. Then proceed to step 18 to attach the floor with screws. When you need to clean out the birdhouse, you can unscrew the floor and clean out the old nest.

**15 Glue the floor to house body.**
For decorative houses, attach the floor to the house body with glue, such as Titebond II or hot glue (see step 9). It is easy to get the top and bottom of the floor mixed up. Be sure to put the glue on the side that fits the bottom of the house perfectly.

**16 Add nails.**
After the glue has set, nail the floor (decorative houses only) with a brad gun or with a hammer and 1" (2.5cm) nails.

**17 Paint the floor.**
Paint the underside and edges of the floor with acrylic paint to blend everything together. I mix Territorial Beige with a little Wedgewood Blue to get this color, and adjust it to match the house body.

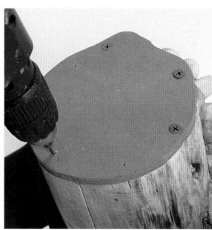

**18 Add the screws.**
For functional birdhouses, attach the floor with screws instead of glue so that it can be removed for cleaning. Start by drilling pilot holes, then insert 1" (2.5cm) screws without adding glue. Four to five screws is enough for most houses. Be sure to put the screws close enough to the edge of the floor to go into the walls, but not so close that the screws come through the wall of the house. Try to avoid inserting screws into any areas in the walls that have cracks or are a bit thin.

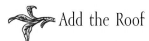 Add the Roof

Roofs can be made from a variety of materials, including fence boards, barn boards, metal sheeting and even metal funnels. Some of these materials are featured in the projects later in the book. This demonstration uses the roof type that I prefer, a shake roof. The shakes measure from about ³⁄₈" (9.5mm) at the bottom for small houses and up to 1" (2.5cm) for larger houses.

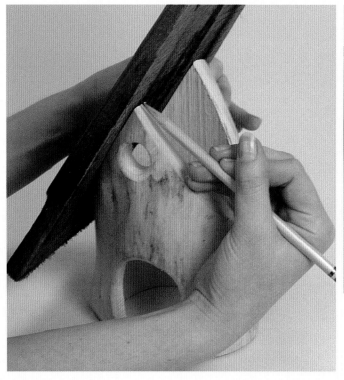

**19** **Mark the wood.**
The first step is to find a shake or piece of flat wood of the appropriate size. There should be an overhang on three of the four edges of the roof that varies slightly with the size and character of the house. A large house might have a 1" (2.5cm) overhang and a small house might have ¾" (2cm). This gnome house will have an overhang of about 1" (2.5cm) in the front and the back and about 2½" (6.5cm) at the lower edge. The shake needs to be 2" (5cm) wider than the house and 3" (7.5cm) longer than the gable or cut angle on the roof. Hold it against the house to mark it for cutting.

**20** **Cut the roof pieces.**
Cut the shake to the length of your marks and round the lower corners as you go. I round the lower edges of the round houses to make the house look more natural. A square house often looks better with a square roof line.

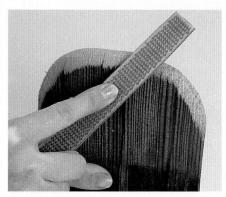

**21** **Round the edges.**
After cutting the shake, use a flat rasp or a sanding block with coarse sandpaper to round the roof edges. A belt sander would be faster, but I enjoy doing this by hand. Rounding sharp edges is one of the secrets for making the houses look natural.

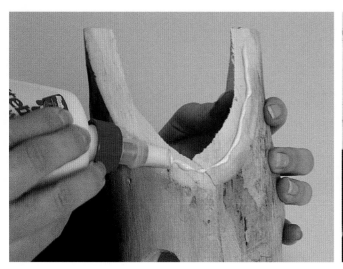

**22 Glue the roof to the house.**
Next, apply glue to the house where the roof will be attached. You can use hot glue as discussed before. For outdoor houses use Titebond II or Liquid Nails construction adhesive. The roof pieces should meet at the gable. They will be trimmed flat later.

**23 Nail the roof (indoor houses only).**
For indoor houses, nail the roof in several places: two nails in the middle of the sides and one at the bottom. Try to gauge where the house body is under the roof so the nails go into the house wall. Use nails that are longer than the thickness of the roof. Be sure the nails do not penetrate into window openings.

**24 Add screws (outdoor houses only).**
For an outdoor birdhouse, you will need to add screws instead of nails, although you can use several brads to hold the roof in place before you insert the screws. I use three 1" to 1¾" (2.5cm to 4.5cm) long screws depending on the thickness of the shake. Again, avoid putting a screw through a window opening and be sure that the screws penetrate into the walls of the house.

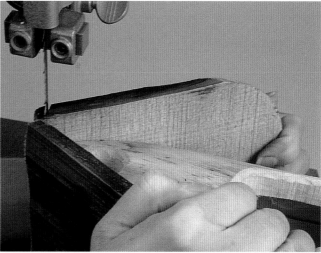

**25 Cut off the top edge.**
Before adding the roof ridge, set the house on its back and trim the top edge of the roof peak so it's flat. You do not want this cut to slant downward toward the front of the house because the overhang would hide the face of the house. Cut it level or angled back a bit. The goal is to cut the shakes where the house front comes to a peak and not cut into the house body. If you do cut into it a little bit, do not be discouraged. Just finish the house and know you will improve with practice.

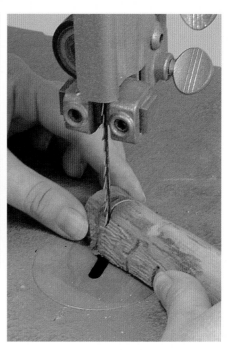

**26** **Cut a branch for the ridge.**
Find a straight piece of limb about 2"
(5cm) in diameter that is a couple of inches
(5cm) longer than the roof peak. For the larger
houses, look for a branch that is the diameter of
a heavy broomstick or closet pole; small houses
will need smaller diameter ridges. You are going
to cut this piece of limb in half lengthwise for
your roof ridge. Try to make this cut smooth and
straight so it will fit well on the house roof with
no gaps to fill.

**27** **Mark and cut the ridge.**
Mark the length of the ridge by setting it on
the house. It should overhang slightly in the
back. The front overhang should be larger, about
the width of two fingers, because you will be attaching a decorative support there. Cut on the
marks with the saw of your choice.

**28** **Sand the edges.**
Use your sanding block or sandpaper to round the cut edges.

**29** **Glue the ridge.**
Apply Titebond II wood glue to the area of the roof where the ridge
will go.

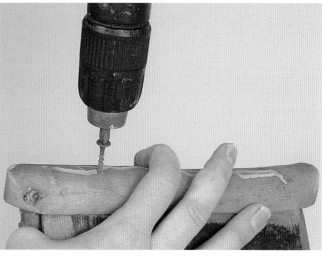

**30** **Nail the ridge (indoor houses only).**
Set the ridge in place, adjusting the overhangs. For the indoor houses, nail the ridge in the front and back to the body of the house.

**31** **Add screws (outdoor houses only).**
For outdoor houses, the roof ridge must be attached with screws long enough to go through ridge into the front wall and the back wall of the house body. It's best to drill pilot holes first. Place your holes so the screw won't come through into a window opening.

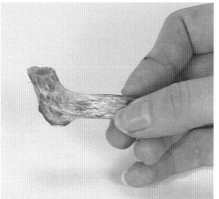

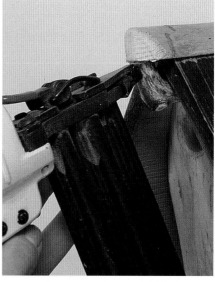

**33** **Fit the piece.**
Then adjust the fit by sanding, rasping or cutting the piece to fit well between the top of the upper window and the bottom of the ridge overhang.

**32** **Cut the roof ridge support limb.**
The last step in the roof process is adding the roof ridge support. This little piece of wood looks like a bent finger in size and shape. Cut the piece at right angles.

**34** **Glue and nail the ridge support.**
This is good place to use hot glue. Apply glue to the top of the support, set it in place and nail it to the ridge. Then glue and nail the other end to the body of the house. When I make very small or simple houses, I put a seedpod or little pinecone in this area. This is an easier way to provide a decorative touch.

The previous page completes the basic hollow log house building techniques. There are many details that can be added to this basic house to create a unique character. This section shows how to make the windows, Y roof supports, the Eyebrows over the door, and the chimneys. Please note that this section does not cover all the decorations for the houses. Porches and porch roofs, window ledges and roofs, steps and seedpod door lights are covered in the individual projects. Your house may include any of these decorative features applied in any combination.

## Add Window Crosspieces

**1** **Cut the twigs.**
To make the window crosspieces, cut two small twigs (about the size of a match) for each window. They should be slightly longer than the window opening.

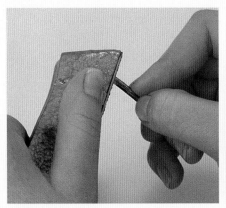

**2** **Sand the twigs.**
Sand the twigs flat on the ends with a slight slant to fit in the round window hole. Keep working at this until the twigs have a snug fit, one horizontally and the other vertically.

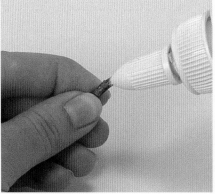

**3** **Apply the glue.**
Apply Titebond II glue to the sanded ends. If your house is an indoor decorative house, you can substitute hot glue if you work quickly.

**4** **Place the twigs.**
Insert the first twig into the window hole deep enough to leave room for the second twig to be placed on top of it at a right angle. Then set the second twig in place.

## Decorate with Ys

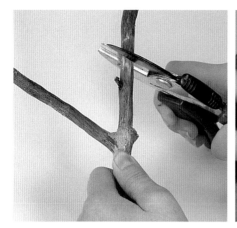

**1** **Cut two Ys.**
Use garden clippers to cut two forked limbs into a Y shape for the roof support decorations, one for each side of the house. You can also use single limbs, as in the Woodland Gnome Home. Whatever the shape, the technique is the same.

*Another way to cut these Ys is on the saw, which is the best way to cut larger limbs that can't be cut with the garden clippers.*

*Whenever I collect limbs, I cut some Ys and place them in a basket so they are ready when I need them.*

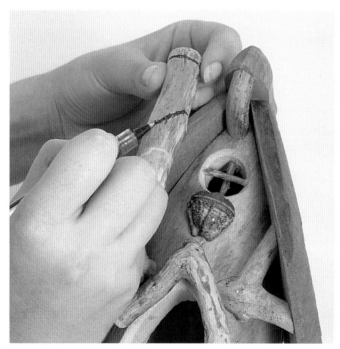

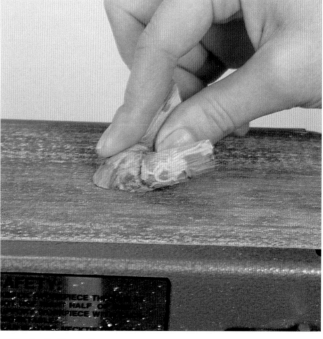

**2** **Mark the limbs.**
Measure the Ys on the house, mark them and cut them to size.

**3** **Angle the ends.**
Angle both ends of each Y 45° to fit against the house body and under the roof eaves. This is a "sand and test" process: cut, rasp and sand the pieces until they fit. This gets easier with practice. You can fill gaps with glue and sawdust as described on page 15.

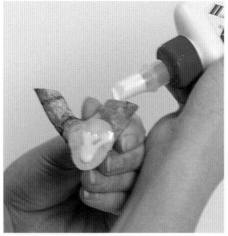

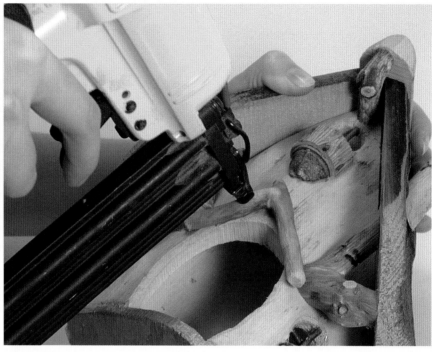

**4** **Glue the Ys in place.**
When you are satisfied with the fit, glue the pieces in place. Where to place these supports is a matter of choice. The upper ones begin at the base of the top window. It's a good idea to mark the location so that once glue is on the twig you can place it without moving it around and smearing the glue.

**5** **Nail the Ys.**
Use brads or small nails to nail the Ys at the base and into the roof. If the upper parts are too small to nail, put only one nail into the base.

This is a good place to discuss the length of brads or small nails. For everything up until now, a 1" (2.5cm) nail would be fine. When you begin nailing the smaller parts, it's better to use a brad or nail that is shorter, from ⅝" to ¾" (1.6cm to 1.9cm). Sometimes this process cracks the wood. Depending on how bad this is, you can either fill the crack with glue and sawdust or replace the twig. If cracking is a constant problem and you're using a brad gun, you may need to lower the pressure of the compressor. I use about 50 lbs. of pressure for my brad gun.

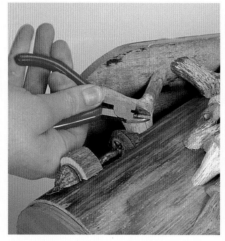

Sometimes your nail or brad will poke through to the other side, or a brad won't go into the wood all the way. If this happens, use diagonal pliers to nip off the protruding nail, then use a punch and hammer to tap it into the wood. This technique can be used anytime you have a nail poking through any part of your house.

28

 Decorating with Eyebrows

**1** **Remove excess bark from a small branch.**
Use pliers to twist and remove any bark that may remain on limbs and twigs. This bent branch will be an Eyebrow over a door.

**2** **Trim the branch.**
Trim the branch so that it fits over the door. If the branch is too thick to cut with garden clippers, use a coping saw.

**3** **Flatten the back of the branch.**
File the back of the branch flat with a rasp. This makes a better surface to glue and nail to the house.

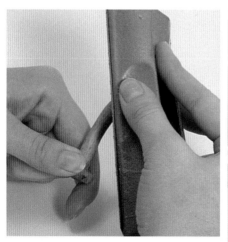

**4** **Round the ends.**
To look more natural, the end cuts must be softened and rounded a bit. Use sandpaper, a fine rasp or a sanding block.

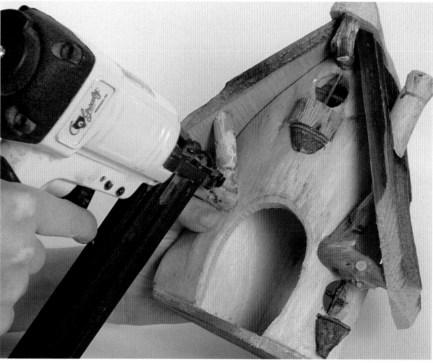

**5** **Glue and nail the Eyebrow.**
Glue is applied to the back and the piece is nailed over the door with two nails. Place the nails in the center of the sides, away from the edges to avoid cracking the branch. You can paint the cut ends with the wood-colored acrylic paint to blend them in.

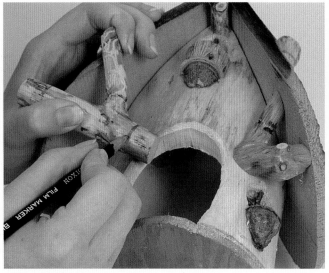

**1** **Mark the branch.**
   Mark a thumb-size branch with the angle of the roof line to make a chimney. The size and length of the chimney are up to the individual. I usually make them about 1" to 2" (2.5cm to 5cm) long.

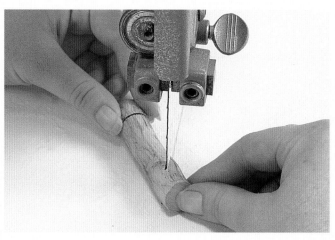

**2** **Cut the angle.**
   The angle is cut using a band saw, jigsaw or coping saw.

**3** **Glue and nail the chimney.**
   Glue and nail this piece in the center of the house roof on whichever side you feel looks best. As always, an outdoor house requires weather-proof glue, but an indoor house does not.

**4** **Add lichen or moss (optional).**
   Lichen or moss can also be attached to indoor houses to add character and age to the house.
   The moss does not hold up well on an outdoor house. Birds tend to pick off the lichen to use in their nests leaving an unsightly blob of glue behind.

Now that you have seen the basic techniques, it's time to look at the actual projects. If you are new at this, the River Rock House chapter (page 32) will give you some ideas that are perfect for a beginner. If you happen to find a hollow log, you'll want to turn to the Hollow Log House project (page 120). The Woodland Fairy House project (page 58) shows more photographs than the other projects. It is small and therefore perfect for learning to core out a limb for the first time. All these houses are original and unique in concept and design. By the very nature of their materials, they are a huge success with our friends in the wild and a delight to those who see them. Don't forget that you can mix and match all of the decorating techniques for any type of house you may wish to make. I hope that you are inspired by what you see here and that you enjoy the process of making these wonderful, natural creations.

# River Rock House

THE RIVER ROCK HOUSE IS UNIQUE in several ways. It is not a woodworking project and so it can be made almost entirely at the kitchen table! In fact, it shares many similarities with cake decorating. Rather than nailing on sticks, you apply soft glue with a spatula and push small rocks into it. You'll probably want to go to the garage or porch for drilling the holes in the pipe, but other than that, this project does not require a shop.

There is something both attractive and nostalgic about a stone house, which evokes images of castles and fairy-tale cottages. Stone is enduring; while wood can perish with time and weather, stone lasts forever. So with careful thought, I designed this house that I hope you will find both fun and inspiring. The base of the body is a 4" (10.2cm) plastic (PVC) pipe that is readily available at any building supply or recycling center (where you might get a piece for free). A 5" or 6" (12.7cm or 15.2cm) diameter pipe works just as well.

The roof is a metal funnel painted with an acrylic patina kit from a craft store. This has a base coat of copper paint and two colors of green paint sponged over it. Alternatives to this would be to rust the metal or paint it any solid or sponged color you like. You can even cover it with small shingles, such as those made for doll houses. I made mine a hanging house, but it would look equally nice mounted on a post or set on a shelf. Best of all, it can be a functional birdhouse; the smaller diameter house is suited to small songbirds, such as wrens, chickadees and flycatchers. The larger house would attract bluebirds and tree swallows.

## MATERIALS

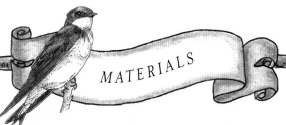

house body: 12"-long by 4"-diameter (30.5cm by 10.5cm) plastic pipe • plastic plug made to fit into the bottom of the plastic pipe (you can buy this when you buy the pipe) • metal funnel 6" (15.2cm) high and 6½" (16.5cm) across • small cap for the top, which can be made from metal flashing or part of a cut-open aluminum soda-pop can • three strands of 16-gauge copper or other wire at least 18" (45.7cm) long • four pieces of wire, 2" (5.1cm) long for the windows • pile of small, flat rocks (⅜" to 1" or 9.5mm to 2.5cm) • large wooden bead (optional, not pictured) • solvent-based construction adhesive, tan or taupe colored, in a caulking gun • fine steel wool • patina kit • gray-brown latex paint • pliers • small spring clamp • spatula or putty knife • Lazy Susan (optional) • siliconized caulking glue (optional) • satin finish polyurethane (optional) • rubber-coated gloves (optional)

### 1 Draw the design.

If you cut the plastic pipe to length yourself, the plastic is easy to cut with any kind of wood saw. Try to cut it straight so the bottom and top do not slant. If you have a miter box, that might be the best way to do it. Otherwise you can draw the cut line on the pipe and carefully follow your mark.

I used a white pencil to draw the design on the pipe. The bird hole diameter is 1¼" (3.2cm) and the windows are ⅞" (2.2cm). The center of the bird hole is 6" (15.2cm) from the base of the house and the center mark for the upper window is 2" (5.1cm) above that. The lower window is offset slightly to one side and is 3½" (8.9cm) from the base.

### 2 Drill the holes.

The plastic is easily drilled with a hand drill or drill press. Hold the pipe firmly because it is a little slick. Wearing rubber-coated gloves will help you hold the plastic better, or a bungee cord can anchor the pipe to a sawhorse. Like the wood, the edges of the drilled holes will need a little cleaning up with a rasp or sandpaper.

 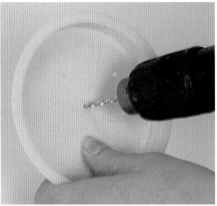

### 3 Sand the pipe.

If the pipe is greasy or soiled, you should wash it with detergent and hot water. Then, wearing work gloves, use fine steel wool to clean around each hole. Wipe the particles off the plastic with a rag. Roughing up the surface of the plastic will clean the surface and help the paint adhere.

### 4 Drill holes in the plug.

Randomly drill about five or six ⅛" or 3/16" (3.2mm or 4.8mm) holes in the cap that fits the pipe. This is for ventilation and drainage in a functional birdhouse.

*The kind of glue you use is very important. I found that the best adhesion was made with a solvent-based construction adhesive, Titebond II Construction Adhesive, but many others are available at hardware stores. It's used with a caulking gun and is strong smelling compared to the latex-based glues. Whatever glue you choose for this project, you will want to get one that's a neutral putty color to resemble mortar between the rocks. Dark brown or white will not look as good. You need to have adequate ventilation when you use this glue, and be sure to wear an apron or old clothes. I also suggest you experiment with applying the glue and the rocks to an extra piece of pipe before beginning your project.*

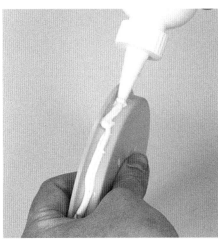

**5** Glue the plug onto the pipe.
Apply glue around the edge of the plug. I am using a siliconized caulking glue, but the construction adhesive used for the rocks will work, too. Try not to apply so much that it oozes out when you put the parts together. The glue is hard to get off clothing.

Insert the plug into the bottom of the house and push until it is set into the opening as far as it will go.

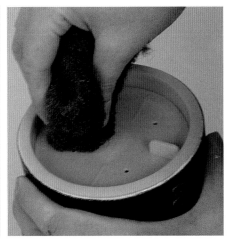

**6** Steel wool the plug.
You can now use the steel wool to clean the bottom the same way you cleaned around the door and window openings.

**7** Paint the plug and holes.
Paint the plug and the window and door openings with latex paint. I chose a gray-brown color that blends with my rocks and with the overall color scheme of the house. You can use any latex exterior house paint that is a brown or tan color.

Set the house to dry in a warm place or dry the paint more quickly with a hair dryer. The paint must be very dry before putting glue on it.

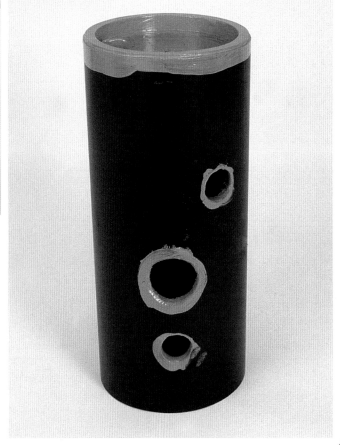

## 8 Drill holes and add wire.

The top rim needs three holes ⅜"
(9.5mm) from the top edge for the hanging
wires. These holes should be spaced equally,
but do not have to be exact. Use a drill bit
that's a little larger than the diameter of your
wire. Put each wire through a hole and fasten
it by twisting it around itself three or four
times. (Note: if yours is a decorative house
that won't be hanging, skip the holes and
wire, and just glue on the roof.)

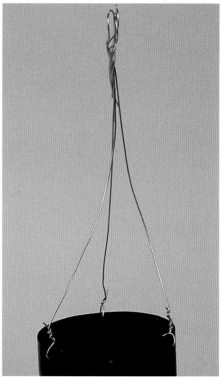

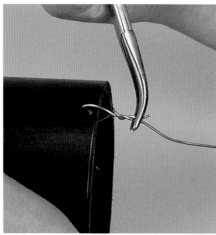

## 9 Twist the wires.

Loosely twist the wires together to keep
them out of your way while you finish the
house. You will untwist them later, so it's
best not to twist too tightly.

## 10 Clean the funnel.

In preparation for painting the metal
funnel, you will want to clean it and roughen
it with the steel wool. You can wash it with
hot water and vinegar if it seems greasy, but
before using the steel wool. Use wire cutters
or tin snips to cut off the spout.

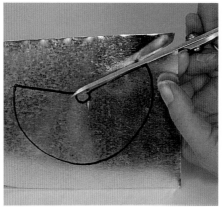

## 11 Make the cap.

I made a 3" (7.6cm) circle pattern for
the little cap on the very top of the funnel. It
is made of metal flashing purchased at a
building supply outlet. You can also cut this
from a flattened soda-pop can. Cut the metal
circle with an old pair of scissors and trim it
to fit the top of your funnel. Another option
is to find a small funnel to use as a cap.

Shape the cone to fit and spread some
construction adhesive along the seam line at
the overlap.

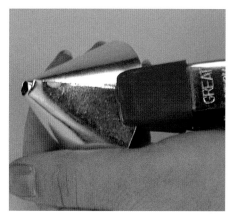

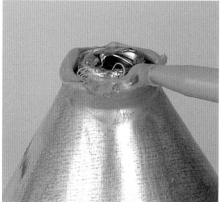

**12** Clamp the cap.
The easiest way to clamp the seam is with a small spring clamp. The glue will take some time to dry, but once dry it will hold securely. (If you like, you can go to step 15 and start on the house body while the roof cap glue dries.)

**13** Glue the small cap.
After the seam has dried, apply the construction adhesive to the funnel where the cap will be placed. It looks good to line up the seams of the funnel and the cap so you can place the seam in the back when you assemble the house and roof. Press the cap into place and let it dry.

**14** Apply patina to the roof.
After the glue has dried, you can paint the roof. I used a kit of three colors that results in a look like copper with a patina. I started by painting three coats of copper paint on the roof and on a wooden bead. Cover them well. Then, I used a sponge to apply the two shades of green that make the patina color.

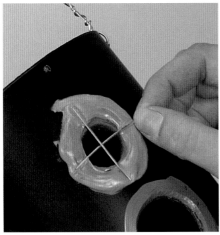

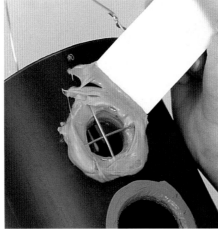

Start applying the rocks.
Cover the ends of the wires with the glue and add another layer of glue. Begin by placing rocks around each window opening. I made window ledges and then outlined the windows with rocks. After you have made one or two circles of rocks around the windows, do the same thing to the door hole, using a larger rock for the threshold.

15 Apply glue and the wires.
Now it's time to begin the house. The first step is to put a ring of construction adhesive around the windows and door with a putty knife or small spatula. It should be fairly thick—an ⅛" to 3/16" (3.2mm to 4.8mm), depending on the size of your rocks. For good adhesion, the glue has to be thick enough to cover at least a third of the rocks' thickness. Since you can't wipe the glue off, I suggest that you practice on a scrap piece of pipe before you start gluing your house to get a feel for the correct thickness of glue.

Spread about a 1"-wide (2.5cm) ring of glue around each window hole and lay the wire window bars into the glue, making them as flush as possible.

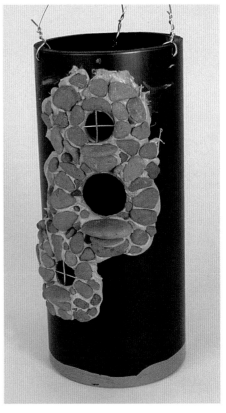

*Notice the pattern the rocks make around the window and door openings.*

17 Spread on more glue.
Now cover the rest of the house with rocks, starting at the foundation. I found that putting on just enough glue for a couple rows at time seems to work best. While the glue takes a long time to cure completely, it gets less sticky to the touch pretty quickly when exposed to the air. Squeeze out the glue then use a putty knife, kitchen knife or spatula to spread the glue evenly over the surface.

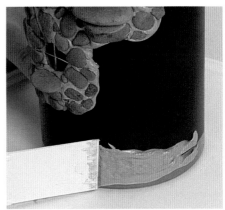

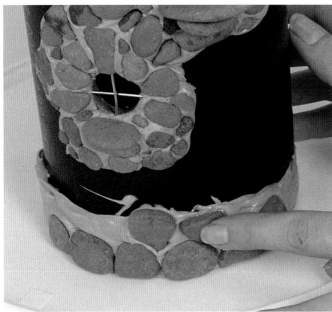

**18** Glue the foundation rocks.
I put a row of larger stones around the base to suggest a foundation. Resting the house on a plastic Lazy Susan makes the process much easier and keeps your fingers out of the glue.

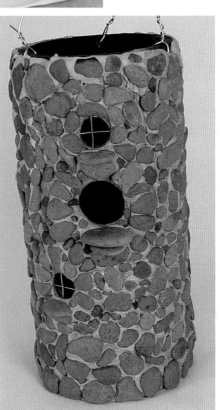

**19** Keep adding rocks.
Keep working on your rows, turning the house as you go. If you need to stop before you're finished, be sure to put rocks in all the areas that already have glue. Then you can pick up later where you left off.

**20** Add the last row.
Keep right on going until you reach the top.

**21** Add the roof.
Now you can install the roof. Unwind the hanging wires, slip the funnel roof over the wires and slide it down to the top of the house.

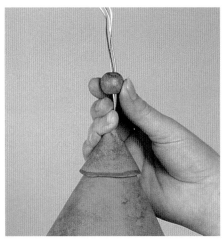

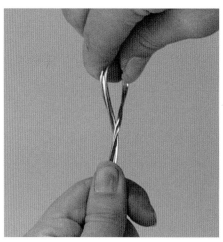

**22** Add the bead.
If you painted a wooden bead when you painted the funnel, slip it on next.

**23** Make a hanging loop.
Make a loop at the top of the wires for hanging. Twist the ends under the loop to secure them.

*Your finished wire should look something like this. Notice that I have not glued the roof to the house in any way. When used as a functional birdhouse, this house is cleaned by lifting the roof. You slide the roof up the wire and empty the contents. The copper wire is good because it's so soft that you can bend and unbend it a lot and it remains easy to work with.*

**24** Add finishing touches.
Here is your finished house—fit for a king. If you want to put this house on a post you can neatly end the wire at the bead and secure the house on a post with Liquid Nails. If the house is for indoors, you can glue three more painted beads to the bottom as feet with your construction adhesive. If you want to add luster to a decorative house, you can spray it with satin finish polyurethane.

**You** *can accomplish a charming and rustic look even without power tools! These two houses were purchased at a craft store and decorated with the same techniques as the River Rock house. Construction adhesive was used not only to apply rocks, but also pinecones, twigs and moss. The twigs were cut to size with garden clippers. The roof on the log cabin was cut out of metal flashing (see the Woodland Bungalow project on page 42) and then rusted . The chimney was made with balsa wood and covered with rocks. The pieces of pinecone used on the round house were taken off the cones with needle nose pliers. It's best to use pinecones that are fully open; warming them up will help them do this. I have used different sizes of pinecones to create a nice pattern on the roof. A redwood pinecone is used for the top knot.*

*See page 99 for a picture of a toad house made with the very same technique as the River Rock House.*

# Woodland Bungalow

THIS PROJECT IS MADE FROM LUMBER available from any building supply store. It could also be made from old fence boards, pine shelving, or any other dimensional lumber that is wide enough. I started with a 6' (1.8m) length of a 1" x 12" (2.5cm x 30.5cm) board. For simplicity's sake, the roof is cut from the same board, and the roof cap is covered with metal flashing purchased at a hardware store. You can also cut and flatten a tall aluminum beer can or use a sheet of copper. The cap covers the ridge where the roof comes together (so you don't have to cut the tricky angle at the roof peak) and makes the roof waterproof. The entire roof can be covered with the metal sheet if you want. If you like rusted metal, the process can be speeded up with muriatic acid. The idea is that this basic design can be made from just about anything you can get your hands on and is meant to be a springboard for your imaginative use of materials.

In addition to changing the materials for the roof, sides and walls, you can create a unique look with the twigs, branches and seedpods you choose. The branches have their bark on them and were cut "green," which is different from my usual instructions. The bark on small branches is quite thin and it dries by shriveling up, so it lasts fairly well. I cut the branches in half lengthwise to apply them. This is not the only way it can be done—you can also work with whole branches. You can sand or rasp the backs of whole branches for a better gluing surface and nail them well. Once the basic house is made and you start decorating, it may be hard to stop! If you make a functional birdhouse, it will attract all kinds of songbirds, such as wrens, chickadees, tree swallows, nuthatches and bluebirds.

## MATERIALS

house body: seven pieces of board for the front, the back, two sides, the bottom and two roof pieces; the front and back pieces are 7" (17.8cm) wide and 11" (27.9cm) high, the two side pieces are 5¼" (13.3cm) wide and 5¾" (14.6cm) high, the bottom piece is 5¼" (13.3cm) square, one roof piece is 8½" (21.6cm) square and the other is 8½" x 9½" (21.6cm x 24.1cm) to allow for the overlap • 4" x 9½" (10.2cm x 24.1cm) piece of lightweight metal flashing, copper or aluminum • about a dozen 5" to 8" (12.7cm to 20.3cm) long finger-size branches, either green or dried wood • square nail, dowel, pencil-size branch or round nail for a perch • two 1" (2.5cm) pieces of utility wire or coat hanger for the window • seedpod or other decorations • waterproof glue (I use Elmer's Squeez 'n Caulk) • ¾" (1.9cm) nails with heads for attaching the roof cap • 1½" (3.8cm) wood screws

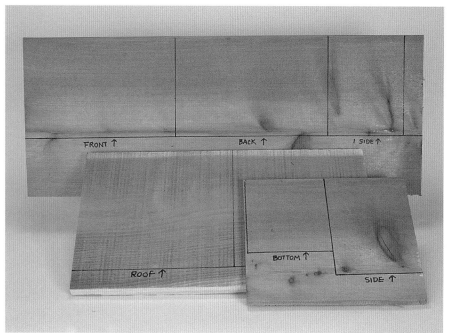

## 1 Cut out the wood pieces.

Draw the pieces for the house on your wood. In deciding what wood to use for each piece, think how the house will look when it's finished. If there is good grain, you might want to place that where it will show nicely. If there is a knot or a crack, you might want to put that on the bottom, where it will not show if it's patched with glue. Always try to work with wood that is not warped or split.

The pieces can be cut with a table saw, band saw or hand saw. Your cuts should be accurate and even to ensure the house fits together correctly. Because the sides are similar in size to the bottom, it might be easy to confuse them. It's a good idea to mark each piece on the back with pencil. Also mark the tops of the side pieces, since their dimensions are only ½" (1.3cm) different in height and width.

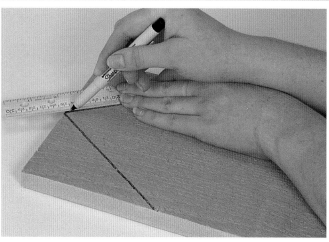

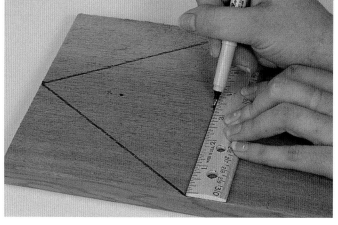

## 2 Draw the gable.

Mark the center of the front piece at the top, and measure up 6" (15.2cm) on each side and make a mark. Then connect the side marks with the center one to establish the gable. Repeat this process on the board for the back of the house.

## 3 Mark the bird hole.

Connect the side marks, find the center of the line and mark for the bird hole. Make a centered mark 2½" (6.4cm) above the bird hole mark for the window.

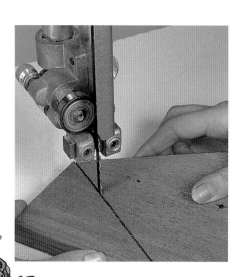

## 4 Cut the gables.

Cut the gable angles on the front and back pieces. Try to make the cuts as straight and as consistent as possible. If you cut in the middle, or to the right or left of your line, try to do that with all your cuts so all your pieces will fit together.

*This house is a very basic style that can be "dressed" many ways—even painted decoratively. Instead of building a basic house, you could buy a simple birdhouse and go directly to the decorating steps. The only drawback is that most of the houses in craft stores are not truly functional in their dimensions, which is important if you want birds to use your house. Of course, if this house is to be purely decorative, you are free to use whatever shape appeals to you.*

**5** Sand the rough edges.
As you work, use a sanding block or sandpaper to smooth the rough edges of the cuts. This will help with tighter gluing and lessen the possibility of splinters.

**6** Drill the holes.
Next, drill the two holes on the front piece. The window is ⅞" (2.2cm) and the bird hole is 1⅜" (3.5cm), which is common for small birds such as wrens and chickadees, and will also allow for larger birds such as tree swallows and bluebirds. These holes can be drilled with a hand drill or a drill press. Place a piece of scrap wood under the board you are drilling and secure the wood well as you're drilling.

**7** Sand or rasp the holes.
Use your rasp or sandpaper from the front side to soften the edges and clean up any splinters on the holes.

**8** Assemble the house.
Before assembling the house, put all the pieces together to see that they fit correctly. It's better to do this now, rather than to find out that a piece needs adjusting when you have everything covered with glue. Put the floor down first, then the front and back and fit the sides in last. Rasp any areas that need adjusting.

**9** Glue the house.
Once the pieces fit, you can proceed with gluing. Exterior glue will require some drying time, but in the long run it is the sturdiest. You could also assemble these pieces with hot glue. However, it's harder to get a really tight bond and you have to work quickly. Exterior wood glue gives you the chance to slide things around a bit. If this is going to be a functional birdhouse, don't glue the floor. Just set it in place.

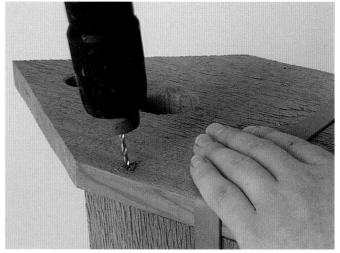

## 10 Clamp the house.
When all the pieces are glued, clamp the house until the glue is dry. I use large rubber bands, but any kind of clamp that will fit the house will work.

## 11 Drill the pilot holes.
Once the glue is dry, you can prepare to screw the house together by drilling two pilot holes on each side of the front. You will be drilling into the center of the side pieces, so keep the drill straight. Drill the holes using a ³⁄₃₂" (2.4mm) drill bit, about 1" (2.5cm) from the top and 1" (2.5cm) from the bottom, on both the left and right side of the front piece.

## 12 Add the screws.
Insert 1½" (3.8cm) screws into the holes. Repeat steps 11 and 12 for the back of the house.

## 13 Attach the floor.
Once the front and back are secured, put two screws on each side of the bottom board. This will be quite adequate to hold it and it can easily be removed for cleaning or you can add a hinge to the bottom and put a screw on the other side.

## 14 Drill the window holes.
This window will be different from the other houses. Four small holes are drilled around the window hole for two small pieces of wire that form the cross bars. No glue is necessary; the penetration of the wire on each side is enough to hold them in place. Use a drill bit that is about the same size as the wire to drill four holes as straight as you can, at the top, bottom and sides of the window hole. It's OK if you can't drill the holes perfectly straight, because you can easily bend the wire. The holes should penetrate about ¼" (6.4mm).

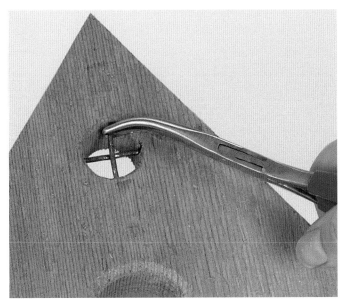

## 15 Add the wires.

Take a piece of wire and poke one end in one hole and slide it in as far as it will go. Then slide in the other end. You may need to trim the wire a bit to fit. Add the other wire going the other direction and you now have a very durable window.

## 16 Round the roof pieces.

Rasp the edges of each roof piece. When I first began making birdhouses, I was in love with English cottages and thatched roofs. I rasped and sanded until my boards were so rounded, they looked thatched. The softened edges take away the "new wood" look and make the finished house very appealing. A course sandpaper, such as 80 grit, will also achieve this look.

## 17 Glue the roof.

Now apply waterproof glue to the gables for attaching the roof.

## 18 Drill and screw on the roof.

Remember that one roof piece is longer because it overlaps the other at the top of the house. Set the roof pieces in place. Drill eight pilot holes and insert the screws. I am brave and just hold the piece in place and set the screw instead of letting the glue dry first. You can tack the roof in place with brads before setting the screws. The overhangs in the front and back are about 1" (2.5cm) and the side overhangs are about 2" (5cm).

## 19 Round off the top ridge.

The roof pieces will not meet because the roof angle is steeper than 45°. This is OK, because the metal roof ridge will hide the gap. Use your rasp, sanding block or sandpaper to round off the top edge of the roof piece so the flashing will fit more smoothly.

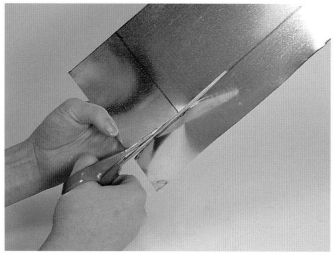

## 20 Cut the ridge strip.
Use a pair of old scissors to cut a 4" x 9½" (10.2cm x 24.1cm) strip of the metal you've chosen. Metal edges are sharp, so be careful.

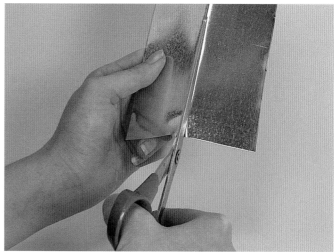

## 21 Crease the metal strip.
Crease the metal strip down the center using the edge of a table or workbench. Then snip each end at the crease so it can fold over the ridge of the house.

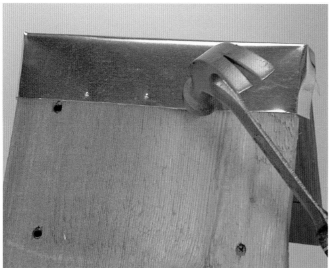

## 22 Tack on the strip.
Center the strip on the ridge of the house so that the overhangs are equal at the front and back. Tack the strip in place on each side with five nails or tacks than are less than 1" (2.5cm) long and that will not poke all the way through the roof board. I use small brass nails that go through the metal easily without pilot holes.

## 23 Overlap the edges.
Tap down the ends of the metal strip with a hammer. The hammer won't hurt the metal and it is much easier than bending it with your hands. Use a couple of nails to hold the ends in place.

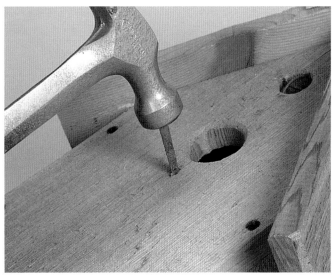

**24** Drill the perch hole.
Since this house is made of cedar, which splits easily, drill a hole for the perch even if you're using a nail.

**25** Insert the perch.
If your perch is a sharp nail that might go through to the inside of a functional birdhouse, file the tip before you drive it in. Insert the perch into the hole and hammer it in until the perch is about 1½" (3.8cm) long.

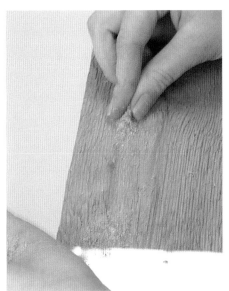

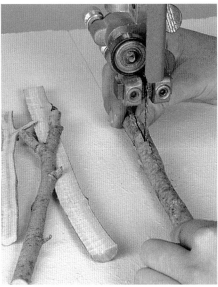

**28** Measure the branches for the front.
Mark and cut the branches for decorating the front of the house. Placing branches along the sides of the front always looks nice—and hides the screw holes—but how you place these decorative features is very much up to you.

**26** Fill the screw holes on the roof.
Fill the screw holes with a dab of glue and a pinch of sawdust. Press the sawdust in a little and then blow off the excess. If the color of the sawdust is too light, paint it with acrylic paint. I only fill holes on the roof because the twig decorations will cover the holes on the front of the house.

**27** Flatten the branches.
To make it easier to add the twig decorations, cut the branches in half lengthwise using a band saw or a jigsaw. (This is too dangerous to do with a table saw.) If you do not have a saw, just rasp and sand the backs to create a flat gluing surface. Don't let the lack of a band saw stop you from working with branches.

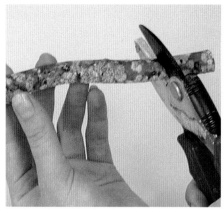

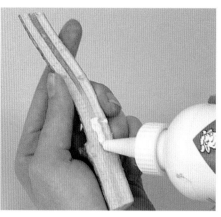

**29** Mark and cut the branches.
The marked branch can be cut with small pruning shears.

**30** Glue the branches.
Spread glue evenly on the back side of each branch, catching the edges where the bark meets the cut wood. The glue actually helps secure the bark, but care must be taken not to apply so much glue that it oozes out when the piece is set in place. If this happens, wipe off the excess glue right away with a damp sponge and rub the area with sawdust.

**31** Nail the branches.
Nail each branch with tacks or a brad gun. This piece required four brads.

**32** Add more branches.
Continue adding branches until you think you have enough. I originally intended to add fewer branches, but the house did not look finished to me until I added more. Notice the two pieces on the edges of the roof. I always add these "fascia boards" to finish off the roof. The wood that I used for the decorations are pruned branches from lilac bushes. The colors contrast nicely with the cedar.

**33** Glue and nail the pod.
I always like to add a seedpod under the window. It is my trademark (or more likely a habit). If you want to add one to your house, first sand the back of a eucalyptus pod until it's flat.

The pod is then glued and nailed in place, right under the window. Your house is now complete and ready for tenants or to enjoy in your home.

*It is simple to make this square house mount on a wall or fence by drilling a ½" (1.3cm) or ¾" (1.9cm) hole in the back of the house and then mounting it on a large nail or screw that is anchored into a wall or fence The hole should be centered and in the upper half of the house.*

**Here** *is an example of the basic house design with an alternative roof and front decoration. The roof was completely covered with the same metal flashing used as the roof cap on the project house. This version is extremely weather resistant and is held on with the same nails that were used for the project house. The rock foundation was applied with the same techniques used for the River Rock House on pages 38–39. The branch trim is typical of techniques described in later projects.*

*See pages 94–99 for a toad house made from the same basic house pattern as the Woodland Bungalow.*

# Tudor Townhouse

THIS HOUSE, MADE FROM A MILLED POST, has a rather urban feeling to it when set next to its tree-trunk cousins. The body is made from a 6"x 6" (15.2cm x 15.2cm) post that is available from any building supply outlet. The best wood to use is cedar, but this example is made of fir because that's what was available. Fir is a harder wood than cedar, so I only recommend using it if you're an experienced woodworker. Redwood also works well. Since the house only requires about 12" (30.5cm) of the post, you can use a scrap post from a building project.

Like the previous project, this is a basic house that can be decorated in many ways. The difference is that this house is hollowed, or cored, like the tree-trunk houses that are featured later in the book. Making this house with a band saw is a good way to learn how to core a house body.

The roof is a shake roof with squared corners and the decorations are pencil-size twigs that are glued and nailed. The twigs can come from your shrubbery, because in this case, it's OK if they are green. I painted the door a soft green with acrylic craft paint to give it dimension and contrast. The roof ridge is made from a square pole, but you can also use a shovel handle or a broom handle. Always keep in mind that you can substitute materials you have on hand for the ones I have used.

This house is suitable for a variety of common songbirds when mounted on a post or hung from a tree or porch. It is also a wonderful indoor decoration, especially if you live in a Tudor-style house.

## MATERIALS

house body: 11"-tall cut from a 6" x 6" (15.2cm x 15.2cm) post (Note: it's called a 6x6 post, but it's really 5⅜" or 13.7cm square because of the milling) • two pieces of roofing 8"-tall x 6¾"-wide (20.3cm x 17.2cm) • 8" (20.3cm) long roof ridge (I used a 1" (2.5cm) square pole cut in half lengthwise) • 6" x 6" (15.2cm x 15.2cm) floor that's about ⅝" (1.6cm) thick (the floor will be larger than the house body) • square nail or dowel for a perch • twigs for window crosspieces • ten pencil-size twigs or small branches that are about 7" (17.8cm) long • chimney from a limb 2½" (6.4cm) long and about 1" (2.5cm) diameter • two small pieces of shakes for porch and window roofs • two seedpods, a small one for a door handle and a larger one for the window • green acrylic paint • clear varnish (optional)

## 1 Draw the house.

Choose the front of the house and draw the roof angles by making a small mark at the top center. Measure down 5" (12.7cm) on each side and make a mark. Connect the marks to make a triangle.

The bird hole is 1⅜" (3.5cm) in diameter for smaller songbirds. It is centered and is 6⅝" (16.8cm) from the base of the house. The center mark for the upper window is 2" (5cm) above the center of the bird hole, and the hole is ¾" (1.9cm) in diameter. The lower window edge is 1" (2.5cm) from the side and 1½" (3.8cm) from the base of the house.

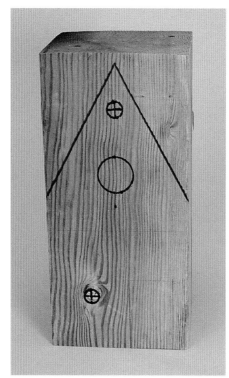

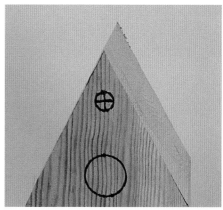

## 2 Cut the roof lines.

I cut the roof lines on my band saw as described on page 18. Remember that if this cut does not come out perfectly smooth, you can rasp and sand it after the house body is hollowed out. It will be much easier to do then.

## 3 Drill, core and add the crosspieces.

First drill the windows using a ¾" (1.9cm) drill bit. Drill the bird hole using a 1⅜" (3.5cm) bit. Then follow the directions on page 19 for coring the house. With this project you can cut into the body and cut all the way around coming out the same way you came in; this makes one glue line. However, if this seems too hard, cut the house in half and hollow each side.

Next, rasp the window holes. Add the crosspieces as shown on page 26. Then glue the halves of the house as discussed on page 20. (This is not a round log, but the hollowing out process is the same concept.)

## 4 Prepare the floor piece.

Cut your floor piece 6"x 6" (15.2cm x 15.2cm) and rasp or sand the edges to smooth and round them.

## 5 Attach the floor.

Place the floor on the bottom of the house body, centering it on all four sides. Drill pilot holes and attach the floor with four 1½" (3.8cm) wood screws. If this is a decorative house, glue and nail the floor to the house body with Titebond II glue and 1" (2.5cm) nails. If this will be an functional house, do not use glue—you need to be able to remove the floor for cleaning purposes.

## 6 Add the roof and ridge.

Refer to pages 22–23 for detailed instructions on attaching the roof. If the house is going outside, use screws instead of nails, so it will be sturdier. Note that I have left this roof with squared corners to match the square house, so ignore the part about rounding the corners. It's still nice to rasp and sand the lower edge, though. The roof ridge is cut in half lengthwise, whether it's square or round. The edges of the roof ridge are rounded and sanded quite a bit to soften the look.

## 7 Add the perch.

For the perch, drill a pilot hole so the square nail doesn't crack the wood. A perch can be a horseshoe nail, dowel or stick. Drive the square nail in with a hammer. I trimmed the end of this nail with a hacksaw because it was over 3" (7.6cm) long, which was too long. The finished perch should stick out about 1½" (3.8cm).

## 8 Start adding decorations.
Glue and nail the window roofs as described on page 79 in the Mountain Gnome Home project. Attach the seedpod under the lower window. Next, draw a horizontal line about 5" (12.7cm) up from the base. Draw a door 1¾" x 2¾" (4.5cm x 7cm) about a finger's width from the corner of the house. Your first twigs go on the edges of the house (see pages 49–50 for directions on decorating with twigs).

## 9 Glue and nail the twigs.
Glue and nail the twigs as described on page 50 of the Woodland Bungalow project. The idea is for the twigs to define the style of the house, to suggest that it is two stories tall, to establish a nonfunctional door and to add some decorative touches.

## 10 Add more twigs.
Add some straight twigs to either side of the bird hole roof and one for a roof ridge support. Continue to add twigs until you think the house looks right. You can go all the way around the house or just decorate the front.

**11 Paint the door.**
To further define the door, add a touch of color to it. I recommend that this door color complement the natural colors of the house itself. I watered down some green acrylic paint to make a light stain that lets the natural wood grain show through. Your paint can be more opaque if you wish.

**12 Add the doorknob.**
After the door paint has dried, attach a doorknob by drilling a hole and inserting a seedpod. Glue to secure. I used a small eucalyptus seedpod, but a wooden bead or an upholstery tack would also work.

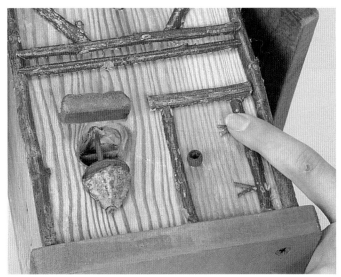

**13 Attach the door hinges.**
Add small pieces of twig to look like hinges. These are glued in place with hot glue for an indoor house or Titebond II wood glue for an outdoor house. If the glue shows a little, rub on some fine sawdust and after the glue dries, touch up the area with paint.

**14 Add the chimney.**
Add the chimney as described on page 30. This house has been sprayed lightly with clear varnish to enhance the wood trim because it is a decorative house. However, the varnish odor sometimes discourages birds from using a functional birdhouse.

# Woodland Fairy House

THE WOODLAND FAIRY HOUSE IS A WHIMSICAL LITTLE HOUSE that sits perfectly on the kitchen windowsill or your favorite shelf. Because of its small size, this house is perfect for getting acquainted with making houses out of logs, limbs and twigs. And nothing is more delightful than a row of these lined up in slightly different sizes and shapes. The Woodland Fairy House can be made from a variety of materials—whether it's a limb that blew down in a winter storm or one salvaged from spring pruning. One year, I saved my Christmas tree and made little houses from the trunk and branches. This house can also be made from balsa wood entirely without power tools (see the picture of this version at the end of this section, page 69). The basic construction of this style house is covered in the beginning of the book.

If it is hard for you to find a log, you can make a cylinder out of a small cedar fence post or a block of balsa or basswood. At the end of this chapter is another fairy house that was made from a birch bark tube. The variety of decorations and building materials are endless, leaving room for your own creativity once you understand the basic building process. Because it isn't meant to be a functional birdhouse, the instructions are for making an indoor decorative house only. If you want the house to go outdoors, perhaps in your garden, you will need to use weatherproof glue and nail it well.

While the house does not invite real birds because of its small size and large door, it certainly invites us to imagine what other little inhabitants might come to dwell there!

MATERIALS

house body: a small log that is about 6" (15.2cm) tall and 3" to 4" (7.6cm to 10.2cm) in diameter (this one is an aspen tree limb) • ¼" (6.4mm) plywood floor • two roof pieces cut from recycled house shakes or shingles about 4½" (11.4cm) wide and 5" (12.7cm) tall • roof ridge made from a 6" (15.2cm) long tree branch • roof ridge support • chimney cut from a 2" long (5.1cm) finger-size limb • bent twig for door Eyebrow • two Y-shaped twigs for roof support • small, short twigs for window crosspieces • small pinecone for door light (a redwood tree cone is used here) • seedpod for window decoration (eucalyptus is used here) • sheet moss for carpet • lichen for roof decoration • acrylic paint

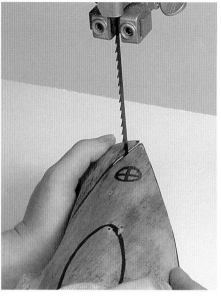

## 1 Draw the design.

The first step is to draw your house design on the log. The window circle is 1¹/₁₆" (1.8cm) in diameter and the center of the window is about 5" (12.7cm) from the base. Rather than measure the roof angle, draw the angle that looks right to you. If this seems difficult to imagine, use a 45° angle or something slightly steeper. The door opening is 2⅝" (6.7cm) tall and 1⅝" (4.1cm) wide.

## 2 Cut the roof angle.

The roof angle cut is made on the band saw. It is easier to smooth this cut after the house is cored because there is less wood to sand or rasp.

## 3 Drill the window hole.

Drill the hole for the window using an 1¹/₁₆" (1.7cm) spade drill bit. The window size can vary somewhat, but if the window is too small it is difficult to rasp the edges and get the crosspieces in. The depth of this hole should be between ¾" (1.9cm) and 1" (2.5cm).

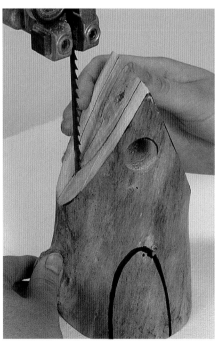

## 4 Core the house.

Cut the house in half as described on page 19 and core it.

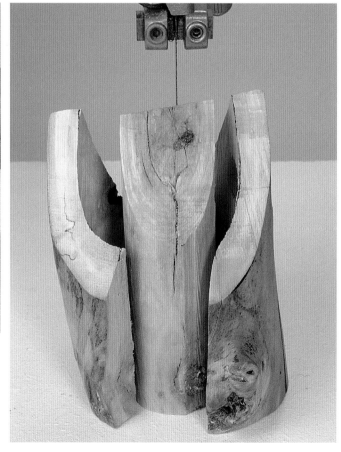

**5** Cut the door and glue the house body.
On the front half of your hollowed house, cut out the door following the drawn lines. Next, glue the halves together as described on page 20.

as described on page 20.

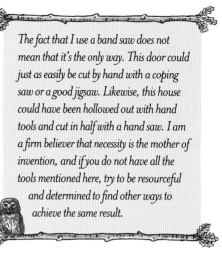

*The fact that I use a band saw does not mean that it's the only way. This door could just as easily be cut by hand with a coping saw or a good jigsaw. Likewise, this house could have been hollowed out with hand tools and cut in half with a hand saw. I am a firm believer that necessity is the mother of invention, and if you do not have all the tools mentioned here, try to be resourceful and determined to find other ways to achieve the same result.*

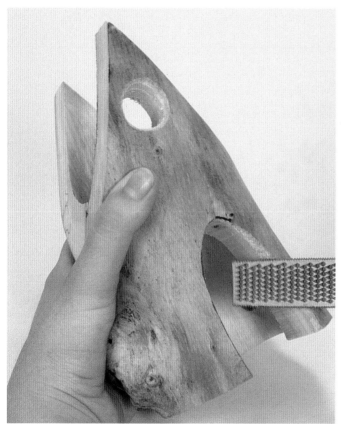

**6** File the edges.
Rasp the windows and doors to take away the sharp edges of the cuts and to make the openings look more natural and worn in. You can also accomplish this by rolling a small piece of 80- or 100-grit sandpaper into the size of a pencil and using it like a rasp. How much to sand or file is up to you.

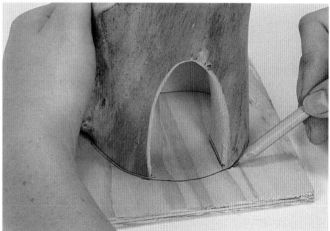

**7** Trace the floor.
For the floor, you'll need a piece of ¼" (6.4mm) thick wood. Trace around the house, and when you get to the door opening, keep drawing as if it were not cut out. You can even add a small bulge there for a door threshold. Mark the door opening to help you position the floor later.

*Instead of a plywood floor, you could use a slab of the log the house is made from, although it is not as durable as plywood. Over time log slab floors tend to crack or split. If your house is for indoor use, this will not be a problem. Covering the floor with glue for the moss "carpet" can have a strengthening effect if you cover it well. You might also use a scrap of paneling, an old drawer bottom or a piece of Masonite. If you plan for this to be an outdoor house, it's better to stick with exterior-grade plywood.*

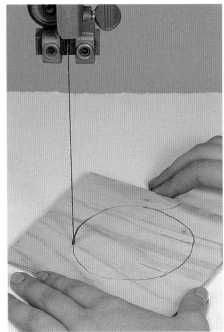

### 9 Sand the edges.

Once your floor is cut, you will want to clean up the rough edges with sandpaper or a sanding block. The bottom side will be the rough one and it's nice to round off that edge a little, the same way you did with the doors and windows.

### 10 Paint the floor.

Now you can paint the floor bottom and edges with a color that's compatible to the wood as described on page 14. The paint blends the color of the floor with the house and seals it from moisture. If the house is going to be in a damp location, several coats of paint will give the best protection.

### 8 Cut out the floor.

Cut the floor. Keep to the middle or outside of your line because it looks better for the floor to be a bit larger. You can sand or rasp imperfections down to size, but it's really hard to add wood where it's missing.

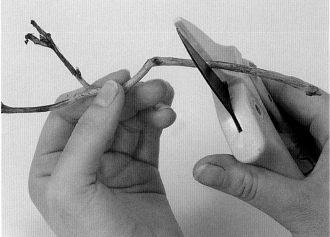

### 12 Make the crosspieces.

For the window crosspieces, you'll want a dry twig about the size of a matchstick. In fact, if you can't find a twig, by all means use a wooden matchstick. Nip two pieces that are slightly longer than the diameter of the window hole.

### 11 Attach the floor.

You can hot glue the floor and then nail it (you have to work quickly with hot glue to get a tight fit), or you can use wood glue and nails or the nails alone to attach the floor to the house body. Use the marks you made to help position the floor correctly.

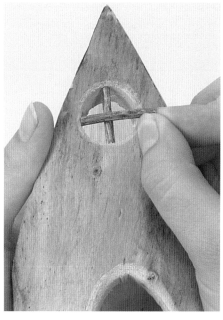

**13** Sand the twig.
Sand the ends of the twig so that they are flat and slightly slanted to make a tighter fit. Be careful not to sand so much that you lose the tight fit. Keep checking the fit as you sand.

**14** Glue the twigs in place.
When you have a good fit with both pieces, apply glue to each of the sanded ends. Set the twigs in place one at a time. The tight fit holds them in place while the glue sets. If you have chosen to use hot glue, it's best to apply a slight pressure until the glue is cool.

**15** Add the roof.
The roof is next. Turn to page 22 for instructions on this process. Now it's starting to look like a real house.

**16** Make the roof ridge support.
For the roof ridge support, select a curved twig that is bent like an L, though it doesn't have to be bent quite that much. It should be about ⅜" (9.5mm) in diameter. Mark the length that is appropriate for your roof ridge and house. Cut the ridge support on the lines, remembering that it's always best to cut it slightly larger than necessary and then rasp or sand it to fit.

**17** Attach the ridge support.
Put the piece in place and sand it until you are happy with how it fits. Apply hot glue to secure it, and while holding the support in place, nail it into the roof ridge at the top and into the body of the house at the bottom.

*It is a good idea to try to keep the size of your decorative twigs about the same diameter. These pieces are the roof ridge support, the door Eyebrow and the Ys that support the roof. This is a design concept that creates a sense of visual harmony.*

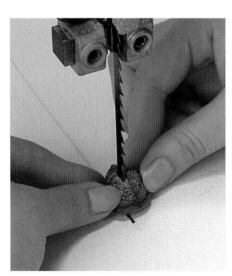

**18** Cut a seedpod.
Cut a seedpod in half to go under the window. This one is a eucalyptus seedpod.

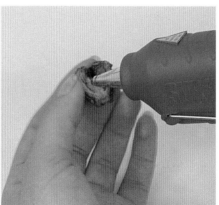

**19** Glue the seedpod.
For this application, I find hot glue is easiest. Apply some glue to the cut side of the seedpod and place it under the window.

**20** Nail the seedpod.
When the glue cools, attach the pod permanently with one small nail.

64

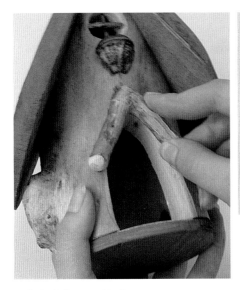

**21** Select an Eyebrow twig.
Now it's time to fit and attach the piece of wood over the doorway that I call an Eyebrow. Look at the size of the twig you have chosen. The length of this piece depends on personal taste, so trim as your own design sense tells you.

**22** Sand the Eyebrow.
Before attaching the Eyebrow, it's a good idea to rasp or sand the ends of the piece to give it a softer, more natural look. This attention to detail gives the finished house the look that it grew that way.

**23** Sand the back of the piece.
It is also helpful to sand or rasp the back of the piece so that it is flat or slightly curved. That gives it a better gluing surface.

**24** Nail the Eyebrow over the door.
Once the Eyebrow has the right fit and feel, apply hot glue to the backside. Place the piece on the house and attach it with one nail on each end. To avoid splitting the wood, nail the twig in the thickest part.

**25** Sand the door light piece.
Choose a seedpod for a door light. You do not want this piece to be so large that it gets in the way of the little twigs that will be placed under the eaves. This project uses a redwood pinecone for this decoration. For gluing purposes, sand the back side of the cone until it is slightly flattened and rough.

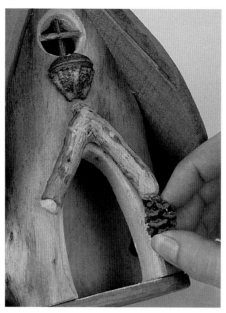

**26** Glue the pinecone in place.
Apply an ample amount of hot glue to the back of the cone. Attach the cone to one side of the door and hold until the glue cools. Remember, even with hot glue, it helps to apply pressure initially for a good bond.

**27** Mark the Ys.
The next step is to mark the little Y-shaped twigs that go under the eaves of the house. Refer to page 27 for more information on attaching Ys.

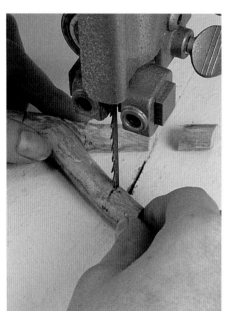

**28** Cut the Ys.
Cut the Ys on the marks you made.

**29** Sand the ends.
Check the fit, then sand the Ys until they fit. The angles of the Ys will vary with each house and piece of wood. It becomes a visual decision about what fits the best. You can always fill gaps with glue and sawdust as covered on page 15.

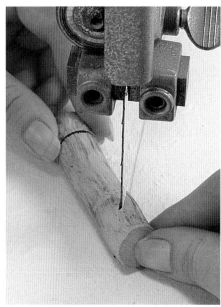

**30** Glue and nail the Ys.
When you are satisfied with the fit, glue and nail the Ys under the eaves on each side.

**31** Mark the chimney piece.
Take the piece of limb that you have selected for the chimney and mark it for length. Also determine the angle to cut by holding it up to the roof.

**32** Cut the chimney piece.
Cut the piece with a band saw, jigsaw or coping saw using your marks as a guide.

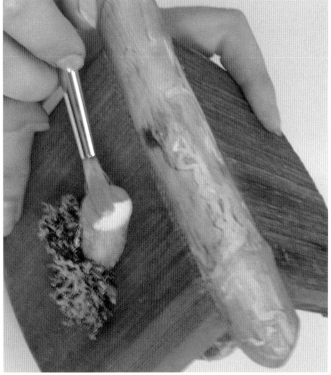

**33** Glue and nail the chimney.
Glue and nail the chimney in place. It looks best to center the chimney on the roof from side to side, but place it slightly higher toward the roof ridge on the vertical line.

**34** Glue the moss and paint the chimney.
For added charm, glue a piece of moss or lichen to the chimney base. Then paint the top of the chimney with acrylic paint so the new cut blends in with the natural wood.

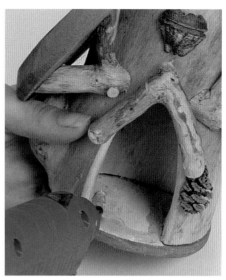

**35** Cut moss for the floor.
Cut a piece of sheet moss that is the floor size less the thickness of the walls of the house.

*Keep in mind that you need a little bit of moss sticking out for the doorway. The moss is very workable and if the piece you have cut is too large, you can press it together to make it smaller.*

**36** Glue the moss in place.
Apply glue to the inside floor, making sure the front edge is well covered. Set the sheet moss in place. Be careful if you are using hot glue. You can easily fill in any gaps with moss. Just make sure the glue doesn't show.

**37** Add finishing touches.
Look over the house and paint any areas that don't blend in. Now you have a finished house that will bring much satisfaction and many smiles.

**This** *fairy house was made without power tools because the body is made from soft balsa wood purchased at a craft store. Balsa wood can be carved with a knife and sanded to create a cylinder. The roof is also thin balsa wood and is completely covered with sheet moss to look like a sod roof. The twig decorations are cut from small willow branches with garden clippers and shaped to fit the house with a sanding block. A little mailbox was added, made from a piece of branch cut in half and a pod for a knob. The awning above the window is a piece of mushroom, also bought at a craft store and glued on. Also, see page 86 for a version of the Gnome-Is-Not-Home house, which does not require the use of a bandsaw.*

**This** *house is made from a small birch tree. In nature, birch trees rot on the inside, but their bark stays intact and lasts a long time. This log was mostly gone on the inside and was easily worked with hand tools. The roof is made from old shakes as on other houses, but you can also use balsa wood. Birch bark "tubes" can be purchased at craft stores and come in a variety of sizes.*

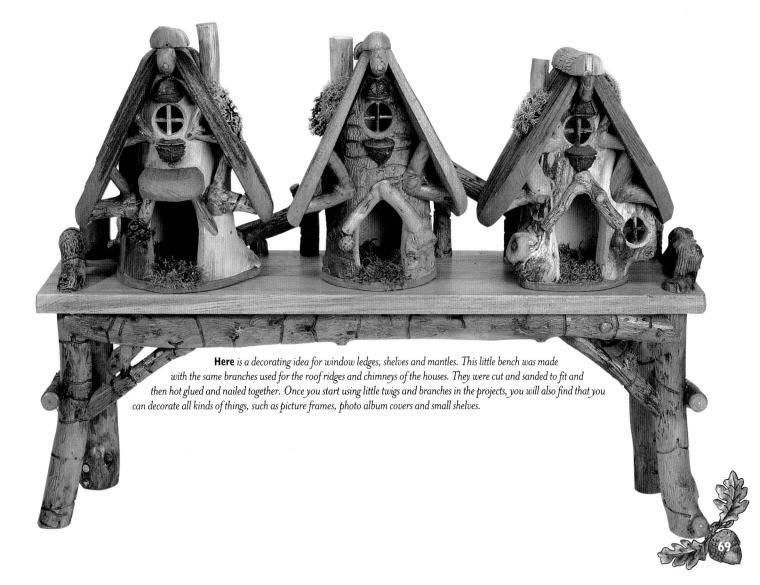

**Here** *is a decorating idea for window ledges, shelves and mantles. This little bench was made with the same branches used for the roof ridges and chimneys of the houses. They were cut and sanded to fit and then hot glued and nailed together. Once you start using little twigs and branches in the projects, you will also find that you can decorate all kinds of things, such as picture frames, photo album covers and small shelves.*

# Woodland Gnome Home

THE WOODLAND GNOME HOME IS IN THE SAME FAMILY OF HOUSES as
the Woodland Fairy House, but it has a more stout appearance and uses more
decorative detail. This is because the gnomes, as a rule, are themselves much stouter
and well-built than fairies and elves, who are oft found airborne and playing in the
treetops. The gentle gnomes spend most of their time working in the earth with pre-
cious stones and caring for wise, old trees. The gnome home is a perfect follow-up project
because the materials are the same ones that are used for the fairy house, only in larger quantities and applied
a little differently. As in the fairy house, the choice of wood for the house body is quite broad, as long as it's a
soft wood that's dry (not green). This is a whimsical, decorative house, not a functional birdhouse. It can,
however, become the home for a collection of little figurines. This gnome home will bring a smile to all who
look upon it.

MATERIALS

house body: cut from a log about 5" (12.7cm) in diameter and 6" (15.2cm) tall (this house is mountain ash) • ¼" (6.4mm) plywood for the floor • two roof pieces about 6" (15.2cm) long and 5⅓"
(13.5cm) wide • roof ridge limb 4" (10.2cm) diameter and about 7¼" (18.4cm) long • roof ridge
support • chimney limb 2½" (6.4cm) long • set of large Ys for the lower roof supports • set of small
Ys for the upper roof supports • two eucalyptus pods for window shelves • half-round piece of branch
for window shelf • acorn for door light • four small twigs for window crosspieces • sheet moss for
house carpet • lichen or moss for roof decoration • acrylic paint

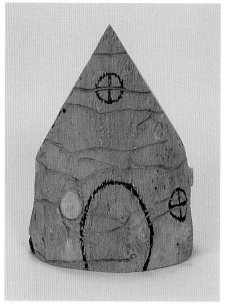

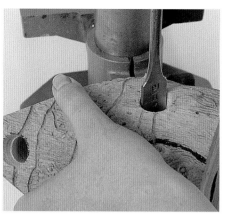

**3** Drill and rasp the windows.
Drill the two window holes using a ¾" (1.9cm) spade bit. Rasp and sand the holes.

**1** Draw the design on your log.
Draw your house on the log. Notice this house has a window centered at the top and another one on the right or left of the door. It's best to keep the lower window at least a finger's width from the door opening and two fingers from the floor, or at least enough space to fit a seedpod underneath. Remember that rasping the windows will enlarge them slightly.

**2** Cut the roof angles.
Next, cut the roof angles as discussed on page 18.

**4** Core the house body, cut the door and add the floor.
Now you can hollow the house, cut the doorway, glue the house body and paint and attach the floor, as described in the Woodland Fairy House project on pages 60-62.

**5** Paint the windows and doorway.
For this house we will use an aging technique. Paint the windows and doorway with the same gray-brown acrylic paint that is used on the floors. This serves to hide the freshly cut wood and also seals the house for added longevity.

**6** Insert the crosspieces.
When the paint is dry, you can install the window crosspieces as described on pages 62–63.

**7** Add the roof and roof ridge.
Now add the roof and roof ridge following the instructions on pages 22–25.

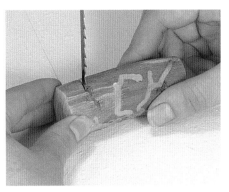

**8** Slice a limb for the shelf.
Now you will be making a little shelf to go under the upper window. Select a limb that is about the same diameter as the window opening and cut a ⅝" (1.6cm) slice off the end.

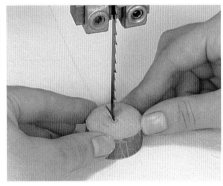

**9** Halve the circle.
Cut the circle in half. Make the nicest half slightly concave to fit on the curved face of the house.

**10** Attach the shelf.
Glue and nail the shelf piece under the upper window. I usually use one nail for a small shelf. If this piece cracks a little, use the glue-and-fill technique described on page 15. If it cracks completely, make a new one that's a little thicker. Make sure that you are not nailing too close to the edge of the piece.

**11** Sand a seedpod.
Now flatten the top of a seedpod with a sanding block. This piece is going under the window shelf as a support, so it can't be any larger in diameter than the window shelf you just added.

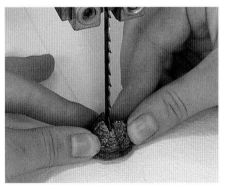

**12** Cut the pod in half.
Cut your pod in half. Now it is ready to fit under the shelf.

*It can be difficult to find a place in some seedpods to put in a small nail. The alternative is to use a very strong glue, such as Crafters Goop or an epoxy of some kind. This will take a longer to dry, but will eliminate the need for nailing the pod in place to secure it.*

**13** Attach the pod.
Glue and nail the pod in place under the little shelf.

**14** Add a pod to the lower window.
Glue and nail a pod under the lower window as the shelf. Because there isn't a shelf, this pod does not have to be flattened on top. It only needs to be cut in half.

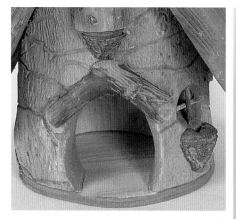

**15** Attach an Eyebrow.
Measure, cut, glue and nail an Eyebrow over the doorway. When picking out this piece, keep in mind you will need to leave room for the Ys under the roof. Attaching this piece is described on page 29.

**16** Add the large Ys.
Next install a set of Ys to the right and left of the doorway to support the roof, as described on pages 27–28.

**17** Add the small Ys.
This house has a second set of Ys that are smaller and placed near the roof peak. There is also a nice place to put these little Ys in the niche at the base of the window. When sizing and shaping are finished, glue and nail them in place.

**18** Add the roof ridge support.
Now add the little bent piece of wood that goes under the front of the roof ridge. Directions for this process are on page 25.

**19** Add a chimney.
Now add the chimney. You could have also done this when you added the roof. Many of these steps do not have to be done in a particular order. As you become more familiar with the process, you can devise your own sequence.

**20** Add the moss carpet.
Install the sheet moss as you did in the Woodland Fairy House project on page 58. Make sure the front edge is glued in place well.

**21** Add lichen to the chimney.
Add lichen or moss to adorn the chimney. If you do not have these materials, don't worry. The house will still be very homey without them.

**22** Make the door light.
To add the acorn door light, flatten the back of the acorn (or other seedpod) by rasping or sanding it so that it has a good gluing surface. Apply hot glue to the back of the acorn and set it in place. Carefully nail the acorn with one nail through the upper part.

**23** Touch up with paint.
Look over your house now and see if there's any fresh-cut wood showing. You want to touch up these areas with your floor paint. Check the chimney top, the window shelf top and the ends of the roof ridge. Also cover any nail heads with little spots of paint.

# Mountain Gnome Home

THE MOUNTAIN GNOME HOME IS THE NEXT-DOOR NEIGHBOR to the Woodland Gnome Home. Since everyone knows mountain gnomes are larger than their woodland cousins, their house is a little taller and larger in diameter. It has more decorative features such as a porch roof, which is a charming addition to any house. Once you get the knack of making the porch roof, you can add one to any house in the book as an alternative to an Eyebrow over the door. This house has three windows and each one has a ledge or window shelf under it and a pod over it to resemble an awning.

This project will show you more ways to expand on the designs you have learned so far. It is nice to make a grouping of whimsical houses in the varied sizes and designs of this and the last two projects.

The log used in this project is mountain ash, a soft wood from trees that grow along creeks. The nice design on the surface is actually made by an insect that burrows under the bark. The decorative pieces on the house are all made from the same wood. There are many other kinds of wood that you can use that are described in other parts of this book. The height of this house is 8½" (21.6cm), which might be too tall to core out using smaller band saws. If this is the case, work with a smaller log that fits your saw, but go ahead and learn how to add the porch roof and window awnings.

## MATERIALS

house body: cut out of a log that is about 8" (20.3cm) tall and 5½" (14cm) in diameter • ¼" (6.4mm) plywood for floor • two roof pieces (these are 7" or 17.8cm square shingles) • chimney limb 2" (5.1cm) tall and 1" (2.5cm) diameter • roof ridge limb 8¼" (21cm) long and 4½" (11.4cm) diameter • roof ridge support • small piece of shingle for porch roof • two porch roof supports • three pieces of sliced branches for window ledges 1⅛" to 1¼" (2.9cm to 3.2cm) diameter • five eucalyptus pods cut in half for window decoration • acorn for a door light • one set of large branch Ys • one set of small branch Ys • one quite small Y for window shelf support • small twigs for window crosspieces • sheet moss for carpet • moss and lichen for roof decoration • acrylic paint

**1** Draw the design on your log.
Draw the house design on your log. This house has three windows that are the same size as in the other projects. The windows can be larger if you have a larger piece of wood, but I would not go over 1" (2.5cm). Remember to allow enough space around the door opening for the cutting and rasping, so the door isn't too close to the windows. Also allow space around the windows for the same reason.

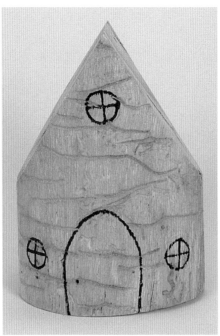

**2** Cut the roof angles.
Cut the roof angles as shown on page 18.

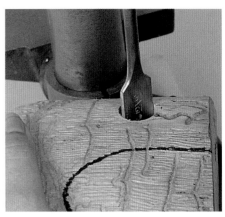

**3** Drill and rasp the windows.
Using a hand drill or drill press, drill the windows with a $^{13}/_{16}$" (2.1cm) drill bit.

**4** Core the house.
Hollow the house out and cut out the door as shown on page 19. Reassemble the house body as described on page 20.

**5** Add the floor.
Cut out the floor and sand the edges. Then paint the edges and bottom with acrylic paint as you used for the Woodland Fairy House and the Woodland Gnome Home. Smooth the window openings and paint them, too. Then make your window cross-pieces. These steps are explained on pages 20–21 and 26.

**6** Add the roof.
Follow the steps on pages 22–25 to make the roof, roof ridge and roof ridge support.

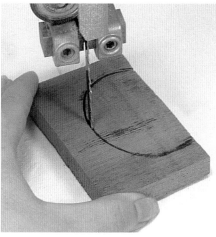

*In most of these projects, I have made the decorative details out of the same kind of wood as the house body. This is strictly a matter of choice, and there are times when I have intentionally contrasted the shelves and Ys. It is not always easy to find smaller limbs that match the large wood. When that happens, you must decide what kind of limbs to use instead. Learn to trust your own artistic judgment about combining and contrasting the wood colors. The house you make is your own creation, and it should naturally reflect your own unique style.*

**7 Add the window shelves.**

Next, create the shelves that go under the windows as described in the Woodland Gnome Home project on page 73. Glue and nail them in place. The shelves look best if they are about the same width as the window or a little larger.

Next, add the shelf supports, made from eucalyptus, acorns or other seedpods, under the lower windows as you've done in previous projects. Later you will add a small Y to the upper window.

**8 Cut a half circle for the porch roof.**

On a piece of shingle or scrap wood draw a shape that is roughly a half circle but perhaps a little fuller. Make it as wide as the widest part of the doorway. The height is about half as wide as that. The porch roof shouldn't hang out too far and block the view of the doorway. You can always trim and sand this piece until you are happy with its fit and shape. I cut this piece on the band saw, but you can use whatever saw works best for you.

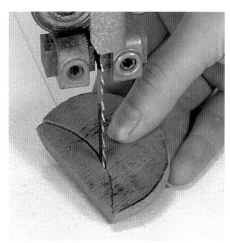

**9 Cut the curved side.**

Next, cut the curved side that will attach to the house. The gentle curve of this cut will fit the curve of the front of the house. Sometimes I also slant this cut very slightly so that it will angle downward just a bit. If you find getting a good fit is extremely difficult, you can always resort to filling any gaps with sawdust and glue as described on page 15.

**10 Sand the piece.**

After the porch roof is cut, rasp and sand the front edge to smooth it and make it look worn and more natural.

**11 Glue and nail the roof.**

Apply glue and place the piece over the doorway, then nail it. You want to make sure that the nail goes into the body of the house, but also watch that it does not come through into the doorway.

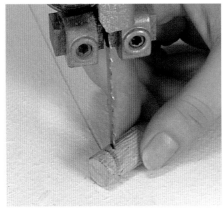

## 12 Make the roof supports.

The next step is making the two porch roof supports. Hold a finger-size branch up to the house and porch roof and mark the angles. Cut the branch on the marks. The angles on these little pieces are about 45°, and the supports will slant in toward each other. Again, getting the right fit comes with practice and observation. Be patient with yourself and be willing to try another set if the first ones are not quite right.

## 13 Sand and attach the pieces.

Rasp and sand the pieces to get the right angle and fit. Then glue and nail these pieces in place, first one side and then the other.

Small roofs such as this can be used over windows as well as doors. The only difference is that window roofs don't need support branches. See the Hollow Log House shown on page 120 for an example.

## 14 Paint the cut edge.

Paint the edge of the porch roof with acrylic paint to blend it in. While you're at it, you may also want to use this paint on the tops of the window shelves.

## 15 Make a small Y.

Now it's time to do the Ys. Pick a very small one that will fit under the upper window shelf. Sand or rasp the back until it is flat and fits well.

**16** Glue and nail the Y.
After you glue and nail this in place, you are ready to add the other Ys and decorations.

**17** Add the seedpods.
I added seedpods under the lower window shelves and over all three windows. An acorn is cut in half and attached to the right of the door for a door light. The decorations you choose depend on the materials that are available to you.

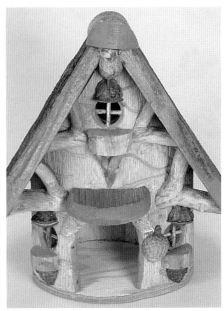

**18** Add the Ys.
Follow the steps on pages 27–28 to add the upper and lower Ys. This little house is starting to look very homey indeed.

**19** Add finishing touches.
The last decorations to add are the chimney, the moss carpet and the moss and lichen on the roof.

Now your Mountain Gnome Home is finished. Each time you make this house, you can experiment with different ways to finish and decorate it.

# Gnome~Is~Not~Home Home

THIS WHIMSICAL LITTLE HOUSE IS VERY CUTE and very quick to make because it is not hollowed out. It is made from a piece of wood that has a natural scar where a limb used to be, or has some other kind of injury to the bark. You may be surprised when you actually start looking for wood how often there is a scar of this kind. The essence of this project is making a house from a log or limb with a closed door created by the natural scar. Usually the scar is an elongated oval that's pointed at both ends. I cut the log in the middle of the scar, and frequently I can make two houses from one scar. If you find a smaller limb with such a scar, you can just as easily make a fairy house with a closed door. The house shown here is made from a fallen oak tree, but you can find scars on every kind of tree.

To make an even simpler house, you can use a scarred log with a funnel for a roof and not need to cut roof angles at all. A house such as this does not require anything but a hand saw or a log cut to an appropriate length. If you can't find a log with a scar, outline a door on the log using cut-and-glued twigs. See page 87 for examples of these variations.

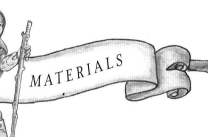

## MATERIALS

house body: a log about 8" (20.3cm) tall and 6½" (16.5cm) in diameter with a natural scar • ¼" (6.4mm) plywood for floor • two roof pieces about 7¼" (18.4cm) wide and 7½" (19.1cm) long (these were cut from old shakes) • roof ridge branch about 9" (22.9cm) long and 5" (12.7cm) in diameter • roof ridge support • porch roof • two porch roof supports • two window roof pieces • two large Y roof supports • two small Y roof supports • three half-round window ledges • three seedpods for window ledge supports (these are eucalyptus) • acorn for door light • small twigs for window crosspieces • chimney about 2¼" (5.7cm) long and 1" (2.5cm) in diameter • lichen and moss for roof decoration • small pod for door handle and tiny Ys for door hinges • acrylic paint

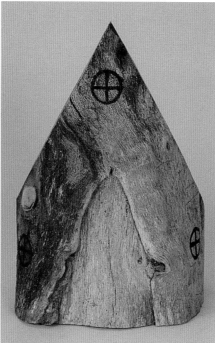

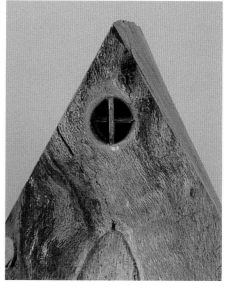

## 1 Draw the design on your log.

Draw the house design on the piece of wood. The size of the house is determined by the piece of wood that you found with a door. Allow enough height for the porch roof, the windows and window ledges. Always remember to avoid crowding the windows and door. This house has three windows that are ⅞" (2.2cm), but if your log is smaller or larger, change the size of the windows accordingly.

## 2 Cut the roof angles.

Cut the roof angles. Since the house will not be cored, rasp any rough places on these cuts now so the roof will fit well.

## 3 Make the windows.

Next, drill out and rasp the holes for the windows. My holes are ⅞" (2.2mm) in diameter. Paint the openings with acrylic paint. (I didn't do this because I liked the color of the wood the way it was.) Install the twigs for the crosspieces in the windows following the directions on page 26.

## 4 Add the roof and floor.

Now add the roof, roof ridge and ridge support as described on pages 22–25. Also cut the floor piece and paint it to blend in with the weathered wood. The directions for adding the floor are on page 20–21. Nail the floor to the house body and fill in any cracks as described on page 15.

## 5 Add the window ledges and pods.

Put the window ledges and seedpods below the windows as described on page 73–74. Paint the cut part of the window ledges to blend them in.

## 6 Add other decorations.

Add other decorative elements, such as the porch roof described on pages 79–80; the lower window roofs (without supports) also discussed on pages 79–80; the upper and lower Ys described on pages 27–28; and the door light described on page 66.

84

**7** Drill a hole for the doorknob.
For the door details, drill a small hole to fit the seedpod you have chosen for the knob. I used a flowering eucalyptus pod for the knob on this house.

**8** Glue the knob.
Choose an appropriate glue and place the knob in the hole. I used hot glue for this decorative house, but you can use whatever glue works for you.

**9** Add the hinge twigs.
Sand the backs of the small Ys you chose for the hinges, then glue them in place. If the glue shows a little, you can dust the area with fine sawdust to hide the glue. The hinges pictured here are from wild roses. They have a nice red-brown color.

**10** Add the chimney and moss.
Choose a side for your chimney, then glue and nail it in place. Add moss or lichen, and you're finished. A cute addition to this house would be a "Gone Fishin'" sign to hang on the doorknob.

*This pine roof gnome home can be made without power tools. It is a small log that had a scar on it that lent itself to being a door; with a hand saw, I cut it flat at both ends. The roof is made from a small metal funnel (you could use plastic) and covered with pine cone pieces using the same techniques discussed in the River Rock House. The window on the door is painted with black and brown acrylic craft paints. The roof supports and chimney are cut from small willow branches with garden clippers, glued on with hot glue and then nailed.*

*This little fairy house is made in the very same manner as the Gnome-Is-Not-Home project, but is charming for its diminutive size. It is easy to imagine it as an asset to any village scene that you might think of.*

**I made this** *little applewood gnome home from a limb broken off an old apple tree. The roof is ¼" (6.4mm) plywood—the same used for house floors—and covered with rusty metal from an old can. It is nailed on with brass nails that can be found at your local hardware store.*

**This** *lovely house was made from a cottonwood tree that fell by a creek. The door is a scar where a limb had come off and then healed over. While birds would readily use this house out of doors, to preserve its beauty it resides on the library shelves!*

# Birdhouse Ornament

THIS PROJECT IS A SIMPLE, small version of the other houses. This little house only sports the appearance of a birdhouse because it is not hollow. It could be hollowed out if you wanted to make it lighter in weight. I used green wood, which makes no difference except to make a heavier house. This ornament is made from an aspen branch about 2" (5.1cm) in diameter, but you can make your ornaments any size you like. You can choose any wood that's available, but I like the look of the light-colored wood against the dark green of a Christmas tree.

This project can be made without power tools. The pieces of branch and the roof angles can be cut in a miter box with a hand saw. You can make a metal roof cut from a flattened soda can or a can lid. Another simple roof idea is to use painted cardboard covered with moss. Balsa wood can be worked with hand tools, such as a rasp and sanding block. You don't even need a drill, since the hole can be a painted black dot. A small brass nail can be used instead of a twig for the perch.

These ornaments can help bring Nature indoors for the holidays. There are many ways to decorate with these tiny houses. They can be hung from cranberry or pine cone garlands or from a hanging grapevine wreath. A bare tree branch secured in a pot can make a birdhouse tree, or you can decorate a small pine tree with these houses, adding mushroom birds and small nests purchased from a craft store. As with all my projects, let these ideas be a springboard for your own creativity. I encourage you to pursue any other inspirations that come to mind.

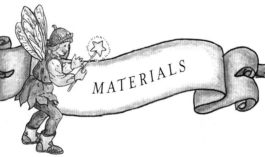

MATERIALS

house body: 2" (5.1cm) diameter and 3½" (8.9cm) tall • two roof pieces cut from very thin wood scraps, about 3" (7.6cm) wide and 2¾" long (7cm) • three pieces of small branch, about ⅛" (1.6mm) in diameter and about 3½" (8.9cm) long (I used willow) • two little Ys for the roof supports • small pinecone or seedpod for a decoration at the roof peak • 10" (25.4cm) piece of narrow ribbon or twine • small twig, matchstick or brass nail for the perch, ⅞" (2.2cm) long

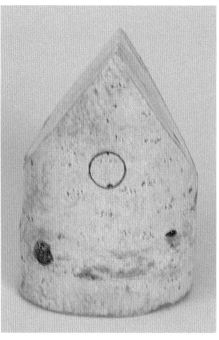

**1** Draw the design.
Draw the design on your piece of wood. The bird hole is ⅜" (9.5cm) in diameter and the center of it is 1⅞" (4.8cm) from the bottom. The roof angle is slightly steeper than 45°.

**2** Cut the roof angles.
Cut the roof angles. This project is small enough to be cut easily with a saw and miter box.

**3** Drill the bird hole.
Next, drill the bird hole with a hand drill or drill press. I use a ⅜" (9.5mm) spade bit, but a standard drill bit will also work. Drill straight in to a depth of 1" (2.5cm). Be sure not to drill all the way through. If you are going to make several ornaments, you can mark the depth of the hole with a piece of tape on the drill bit. Paint the inside of the hole a dark brown or black to give the illusion of greater depth.

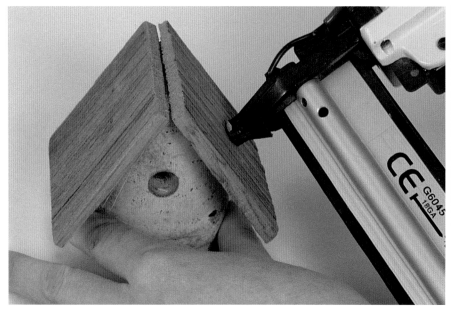

**4** Add the roof.
The roof pieces should have about a ½" (1.3cm) overhang in the front and back, and a little more at the bottom. I hot glue these pieces on and then use a couple of brads to secure them. Since it's an ornament, you can just glue it with hot glue or contact cement. Don't overlap the pieces at the top.

**5** Flatten two sticks.
Flatten the backs of two of your three small twigs to make a good gluing surface.

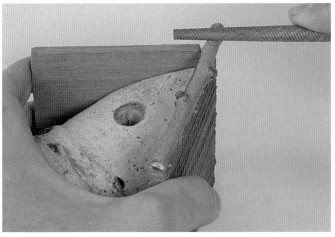

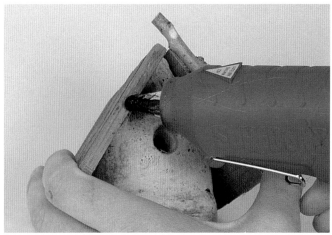

### 6 Glue the first stick.

Glue one stick to the roof line, flush with the bottom. Then make a groove in it where the second one will pass over it. (This is a log cabin technique.) Use a small rat-tail file or a small roll of sandpaper to create a depression, which does not have to be perfect. Any gaps can be filled with that wonderful cure for all cracks and gaps—glue and sawdust (see page 15).

### 7 Attach the second stick.

Apply glue to the other roof face and attach the second little stick, letting it cross the first one at the top. This creates the charming look of a tiny chalet.

### 8 Trim the sticks.

When the glue is set, use nippers to trim the two sticks to an even length at the top.

### 9 Mark and cut the third stick.

Take the third straight stick and mark the length of the roof ridge on it. This can be the exact length or a bit longer, but be sure it is not shorter. Cut the stick with your garden clippers.

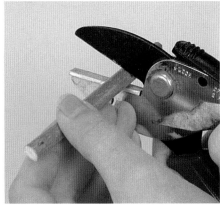

*I often use green or living twigs and branches for these little projects because they can be nailed without cracking and are easily cut with nippers. As the wood dries, it just wrinkles up a little bit. What you have to watch for is that hot glue sometimes does not get a good hold on green wood, especially if it is damp or cold. If the glue does not hold the first time, it is easy to peel it off and apply it again; for some reason, it often holds better the second time. Applying pressure to the piece while the glue cools always results in a better bond.*

**10** Glue on the ribbon and ridge piece.
Fold the ribbon in half lengthwise to find the middle. Use a dot of glue to hold it in place on the roof ridge. I usually place this ribbon a bit towards the front, rather than exactly in the middle. The front of the ornament is heavier and it looks nice with its face tilting upward ever so slightly. When the ribbon is in place, apply a bead of glue and then add the twig for the ridge piece. Press it firmly in place until the glue is set.

**11** Hang it up.
Check to see if you like how the ornament hangs. Add a couple of brads to the ridge if you want, but be careful not to crack the wood.

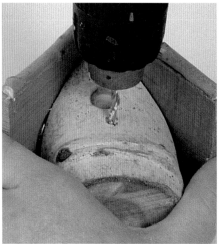

**12** Drill the perch hole.
Drill the hole for the perch using a drill bit that is the same size as the perch twig or matchstick. As I mentioned, an alternative is a small tack or brass nail that can be hammered in without making a pilot hole.

**13** Add a perch.
Apply glue into the hole and press the perch in place.

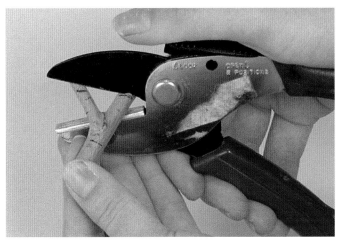

## 14 Attach the Ys.

Now it's time to attach the decorative Ys for roof supports. These need to be cut to a suitable length to fit from the body of the house to the eaves at about the level of the bird hole. Since these are purely decorative and small, they don't have to fit perfectly, just so they look neat and fit tightly enough for good gluing. Glue these in place with hot glue and hold until the glue is set.

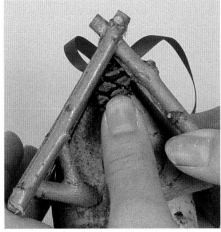

## 15 Add the seedpod.

Apply glue to the back of your seedpod or small pinecone and attach it to the front gable peak of the ornament, holding it until the glue is set.

*Here is your finished ornament—ready to hang. Just think of all the little variations you can create to make a set of these charming ornaments for a small tree or garland.*

# Cottage Toad House

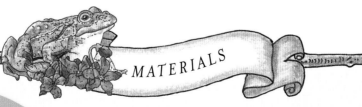

THIS TOAD HOUSE IS NOT ONLY ONE OF MY FAVORITE SUBJECTS, but also the one house most likely to draw comments and stories from those who see it. Over the years, I've discovered that many people have both love and respect for the friendly toad. They help keep gardens free from pests in a most environmentally-friendly way. One toad will eat about 3,000 bugs a month. Cutworms, earwigs, slugs, flies, cabbage moths, snails, spiders and mosquitoes are some of the favorites of this gardener's friend. Before there were pesticides, every horticulturist had pet toads (and encouraged birds for the same reason).

There is just something very amiable about toads. They are a little slower and plumper than their frog cousins. Unlike frogs, they do not live in water, though they do lay their eggs in water. And, for goodness sakes, you can't get warts from a toad. They have glands that are toxic to anything that eats them—it's one of their few defenses. So if I have managed to convince you to love a toad, maybe you would like to make a home for him or her.

Once they have established a home, toads will return every spring. (They hibernate in winter by burrowing into the ground.) They need access to water in which to soak because they drink by absorbing water through their skin. I like to put a shallow saucer of water embedded in the ground near their house in a damp, shady spot.

This project is similar to a gnome home without a floor—so the toad can burrow into the soil. The house should be made as weatherproof as possible. Use exterior glues and screws instead of just nails for the roof. Several coats of paint or sealer protect the bottom of the log. This house is made from a log, but you can also make a toad house from flat boards like the Woodland Bungalow, but without the bottom and with a cutout door. The body of the house is best made from a wood that holds up well outdoors, such as redwood or cedar. If you use other wood, plan to coat the exterior with a clear water-based exterior sealer.

## MATERIALS

house body: about 6" to 7" (15.2cm to 17.8cm) in diameter and 8" to 9" (20.3cm to 22.9cm) tall • ¼" (6.4mm) exterior plywood for the horseshoe-shaped floor • two roof pieces 9" (22.9cm) square • roof ridge branch, 10½" (26.7cm) long and 5 to 5½" (12.7cm to 14cm) in diameter • roof ridge support • porch roof • two porch roof supports • branch for chimney about 1¼" (3.2cm) in diameter and 3" (7.6cm) long • pair of large Ys • pair of small Ys • half-round shelf for window ledge • seedpod for window ledge support • acorn for door light • 3" (7.6cm) long, thumb-size branch for sign (optional) • exterior varnish (optional) • acrylic paint

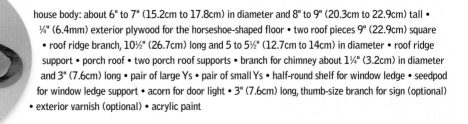

**1** Draw the design.
Draw your house on the wood. The door can be a little wider and shorter than you would draw for a gnome home. The door on the project house is about 3" (7.6cm) at the widest point and 3½" (8.3cm) tall. The upper window is a little larger than 1" (2.5cm) and is placed low enough not to crowd the top, the center being about 2⅛" (5.4cm) from the peak. The center of the lower window is 2¼" (5.7cm) from the bottom and 1⅝" (4.1cm) from the door. I placed the window on the left because of the knot on the other side. Notice how the knot balances the window; this is how natural features of the wood can be incorporated into the design.

**2** Cut the roof angles.
Cut the roof angles as shown on page 18. Remember that if these cuts do not come out perfectly smooth or straight, you can sand, rasp or trim them much more easily after the house has been cored.

**3** Core the house and make a door.
First drill the windows (see page 18). Then core the house (see page 19). I make the walls on toad houses nice and thick—about 1" (2.5cm). Next, cut out the door. Glue and nail the house back together, using exterior glue if you intend to put the house outside. Rasp the windows and the door, then paint them. Painting is especially recommended for outdoor use because the paint acts as a moisture barrier.

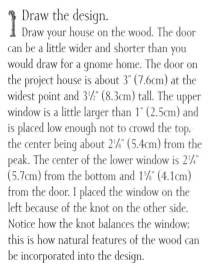

**4** Trace the house.
Trace the bottom of the house, inside and out, for the base on a piece of exterior plywood. You need to make this an exact drawing of the base of the house, which will be a horseshoe shape. Mark the side that goes up so you don't attach it the wrong way.

**5** Cut the base piece and spread the glue.
Cut out the base piece. Apply exterior glue to the house bottom, spreading the glue evenly with a foam brush. The glue helps to weatherproof the house.

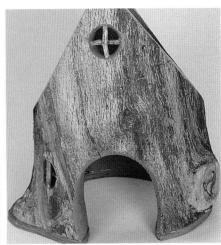

6 Nail the base in place.
The base can be nailed on using an ample number of nails to secure the house and plywood together well.

7 Paint the base and interior.
To make the house more waterproof, paint the bottom and the interior of the house with three coats of paint. This may seem tedious, but a house made from wood that sits on the ground in the garden has a hard life. The better it is protected, the longer it will last.

8 Make the crosspieces.
After the paint is dry, the window crosspieces can be put in. Wire windows might be more durable, but you can use wood as I did here. Installing wire window pieces is shown on pages 46–47 in the *Woodland Bungalow* project.

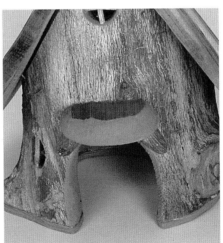

9 Add the roof.
Now add the roof, roof ridge and roof ridge support as described on pages 22–25. It is as important to use both exterior glue and screws on this roof as it is for an outdoor birdhouse. This adds durability and helps keep the roof from warping from constant exposure to water and sun.

10 Make the porch roof.
Add the porch roof as described on page 79 and paint the cut edges.

11 Add a window shelf and pod.
Add the window shelf and the pod support as described on pages 73–74. Notice how the wood contrasts with the dark house body. Remember to leave room for a sign over the porch roof. The best thing is to find the piece of wood for the sign and see how it will fit with the window decorations before you attach them.

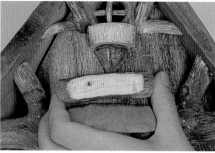

**12** Add the Ys.
Add the large and small Ys. Place the bottom of the large Ys about level with the top of the door. The bottom of the small Ys should be level with the bottom of the upper window. Leave room for your sign over the porch roof when placing these pieces. If Ys are not available, you can cut a support from a branch as we'll see in the Acorn Wren House on page 105.

**13** Cut and sand wood for the sign.
The sign is made from a thumb-size branch cut to the length of the porch roof or slightly smaller. The front is sanded, rasped or whittled to reveal the light color of the wood and to make it smoother and flatter for painting. Leave a little of the natural wood showing on the edges. The small round rasp that is used on windows is good for this task. Sand the back flat so that it can be glued and nailed.

**14** Paint the sign.
I like painting "Toad Hall" on my houses, but you can paint "Welcome" or a different name for the house. Draw the words in pencil and then paint them with a small pointed brush and acrylic paint. A waterproof pen will also work, but it is more likely to fade. Spray the finished sign with an exterior varnish to protect it.

**15** Glue and nail the sign.
After the varnish dries, glue, then nail the sign to the front of the house. If you like this idea, you may want to make house signs for your other projects as well.

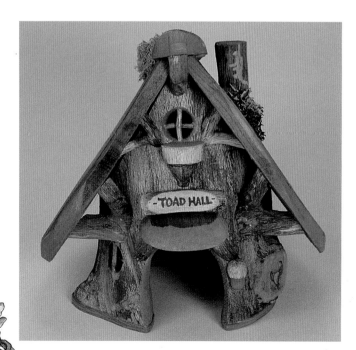

**16** Add chimney and moss.
Last, add the acorn and chimney as shown on pages 30 and 75. I always wait to put the chimney on last to decide which side to put it on. In this case, I felt that placing in on the right side balanced things out. It must be glued with exterior glue and nailed really well.

I have also added moss to the roof of this house because it adds a lot of character to an indoor house. If your house is to go outside, the moss will fall off or the birds will steal it.

Now you have a toad home, and a charming home it is—wherever you choose to put it.

**Here** are two alternative designs for toad homes that do not require a band saw to make. The round one is made just like the River Rock House and does not require power tools, although having a cordless drill to add the round window is handy. The round house is made from a common valve box (as pictured) used in home irrigation systems. It is available at any home and garden store and costs a few dollars. I shortened it some and used the hole it came with for the door. I covered the back hole with a piece of black plastic cut from a plant pot. The roof is made from a large funnel and rusted to look old. The decorative cap was cut with scissors from the metal flashing material (see the River Rock House or Woodland Bungalow project). The square house uses the basic design from the Woodland Bungalow birdhouse. The window is the same size as the bird hole, but raised up an inch or so. The door is cut with a coping saw, keyhole saw or sabre saw before the house is assembled.

# Acorn Wren House

THIS IS A HIGHLY FUNCTIONAL BIRDHOUSE. The birds love it because it looks like their natural habitat; people like its charming, whimsical character. As the title suggests, this house attracts all kinds of wrens, along with chickadees and tit-mice. The reason these little songbirds like this house is the size of the door hole and the size of the interior of the house. Over many years of selling this style house, my customers have told many stories of its success. One woman sent an Acorn Wren House to her grandson who hung it on the porch of his seventh-story apartment in New York City. He was delighted that a wren moved in right away. Another customer who lived in the mountains hung her house on her deck one Easter morning and only an hour later she watched a wren family move in. So you can see why I highly recommend this house for the bird enthusiast who wants a functional house. Of course, this house is also charming on top of kitchen cabinets.

This house is cut from a soft wood log—I used mountain ash—or piece of post that is about 6" (15.2cm) in diameter. The interior cavity should be a minimum of 4" (10.2cm), with walls that are about 1" (2.5cm) thick. The height can vary, but it's best to start with a piece of log that is 8" or 9" (20.3cm or 22.9cm) tall. The height of this house is determined by the cutting height of your band saw. You should make yours as tall as your saw will allow, even if it is not as tall as this example. All the variations of decoration and roof materials that are covered throughout this book can be applied to this basic design, so the possibilities for variation are countless. Although the project house is made to hang from a tree or hook, it can be mounted on a post instead.

If you do not have a band saw, you can look for a hollow piece of log that's the right size for this project. You can also make a functional birdhouse from plastic pipe, as shown in the River Rock House, and experiment with different ways to decorate it to give a natural look.

## MATERIALS

house body: log or post 6" (15.2cm) in diameter and 8" to 9" (20.3cm to 22.9cm) tall • ¼" (6.4mm) exterior plywood for floor • two roof pieces about 2" (5.1cm) wider than the log (these are 7½" or 19.1cm square cedar shakes) • roof ridge, about 8¾" long (22.2cm) and 4½" (11.4cm) diameter • roof ridge support • chimney, 1" (2.5cm) in diameter and 3" (7.6cm) long • Eyebrow to go over the bird hole • two roof supports • one half-round porch • one half-round step • two acorns or other seedpods for porch and step supports • twigs for window crosspieces • size 8 screw eye for hanging device • 24" (61cm) sisal rope • acrylic paint

When you look at your log to decide which side to make the front, you will want to be sure that the house sits level or is tilted back slightly. Notice that my log actually bends slightly to the right, which I think gives the house some character. Notice also that once it is cut out, the curve is not really noticeable, because that part is cut off with the roof angle cut. When you're just starting to make these houses, it's easier to work with wood that is quite regular, but with time and practice you will find that wood with more character makes more interesting houses. Avoid making a house that bends forward. After the roof is put on it will hide the face of the house.

### 1 Draw the design on the log.

Draw the house design on the log. The point of the gable is about 9" (22.9cm) from the bottom of the house. The roof angle is about a 55° angle; I don't measure the angle, but rather simply cut so that it looks right to me. The bird hole is 1⅛" (2.9cm) in diameter, which is the perfect size for wrens and small songbirds. The bird hole is about 5" (12.7cm) above the floor and the ⅞" (2.2cm) diameter window is about 1¾" (4.5cm) from center to center above the door hole. As you plan the design, leave enough room for the decorations you will be adding. Keep the design centered under the roof gable and don't crowd the edges or put the holes too close together.

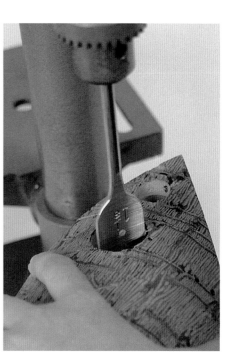

### 2 Cut the roof angles.

Cut the roof angles as described on page 18. You can rasp and sand these cuts more easily after the house has been cored.

### 3 Drill the bird and window holes.

Next, drill the bird hole with a 1⅛" (2.9mm) spade bit, and the window hole with a ⅞" (2.2cm) spade bit.

**6 Rasp the holes.**
Smooth the window and bird holes with a small wood rasp or a piece of rolled coarse sandpaper.

**4 Core the house.**
Core the house as shown on page 19.

**5 Glue and nail the house body.**
After it has been cored, the house can be glued and nailed back together, taking care that the two halves are even on the bottom and no glue is showing. If you plan to use this house outdoors, use an exterior glue such as Titebond II.

**7 Paint the holes and add twigs.**
Paint the window and bird hole edges with the acrylic paint that you have used in other projects. For a functional birdhouse, painting these openings protects them from the weather and prevents cracking. It also makes the house look more finished. After the paint is dry, add the window crosspiece twigs as described on page 26.

**8 Add the porch and step.**
Attaching the porch and step is similar to making window shelves as shown on page 73. The porch should be a circle of wood slightly larger than the bird hole, which is cut in half and curved to fit the house face. The step is smaller, about the size of the window, and is also curved to fit the house. Leave room for the roof supports under the eaves in front. I place the porch no more than $1/8$" (3.2mm) below the hole. The distance between the step and the porch should be about the same as the thickness of the step. The step should be positioned a little to the right or left, whichever you think looks best. Glue and nail these pieces in place.

103

## 9 Add the seedpods.

Seedpods or acorns are placed under the step and porch. To make them fit, cut the acorns in half and then cut a small piece off the ends. If you are working with something softer, you can also rasp or sand it to fit. Glue and nail the pieces in place.

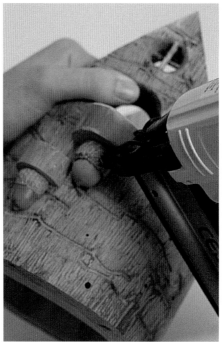

## 10 Add the Eyebrow.

You can now cut, file and attach the Eyebrow over the doorway as described on page 29.

*This is how your house will look with the window, porch and step, and door detail finished. Next you will add the roof, roof ridge, roof ridge support and the floor.*

## 11 Add the roof and floor.

Now the house is really taking shape. Add the roof, roof ridge and support and floor as described on pages 20–25. It's worth mentioning again that for an outdoor house, use an exterior glue. Also, for a functional birdhouse, attach the floor with screws only (and no glue) so you can remove it for cleaning.

## 12 Cut the roof supports.

Next, you'll add the tree limb roof supports. The diameter of your limb should be about thumb size, depending on the size of the house. It fits between the roof and the front of the house and is about 2" (5cm) long. Start by sanding or cutting about a 45° angle on each end. Then sand or rasp the ends to fit. Notice that these supports are not Y-shaped but straight, which is easier than a Y to fit to the house.

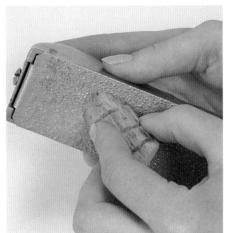

## 13 Attach the supports.

Placement of these supports looks best if placed at the level of the porch. Before attaching any piece to the house, you should spend a few minutes moving it around to see where it should go. You can even decide to add more than one set of supports.

## 14 Add the chimney.

As with other house parts, the placement of the chimney depends on what looks best to you. Often it looks the best on the same side as the porch step. If your house leans a little or has a knob on the one side, it might look best on the opposite side. You will get a feel for balancing the design of your houses as you make more of them. Be sure to glue and nail the chimney well so it won't fall off if it is bumped.

*Notice the placement of the roof supports.*

**15** Drill a hole in the roof ridge.
If you plan to display your house or attach it to a post, you can stop here. Otherwise, drill a hole that's the size of the screw eye you want to use. Holes should never be larger in diameter than the inside of the threads, or the smallest part of the screw. To make the house hang level, position the hole slightly to the front of the center of the roof ridge because there is more weight on the front of the house.

**16** Add glue to the hole.
Fill the hole with a good exterior glue or silicone. Try not to use so much that excess glue comes out when the screw is put in. If it does, wipe off as much as you can and cover the rest with sawdust to blend it in.

**17** Insert the screw eye.
I use a no. 8 screw eye because it fits my sisal rope. After starting the screw, use an old file or other tool to twist it. The screw eye should end up parallel to the roof ridge so that the rope can go through it sideways.

**18** Add the rope.
Cut a length of rope that is 2' (61cm) or a little less. Sisal rope can be hard to tie. You will need a little extra that can be cut off after the knot is tied. Thread the rope through the screw eye and tie your favorite knot.

*Your finished house is ready for occupancy.*

**These** are two variations of wren houses. The one above is a little house with two windows and a fish over the door for fun. I call these "fishing houses." The fish is made from a soft wood and painted with acrylics. The second little house is made from a cedar firewood log and, although very simple, it will attract a family very quickly once it is hung outside. Wrens are very friendly and will nest near human habitations. You can hang a house like this right on your porch or eave and they will be glad to use it.

# Woodland Songbird House

THIS IS THE MOST VERSATILE HOUSE YOU CAN MAKE because it attracts a broad range of small- and medium-size songbirds. Small birds seem to have no problem using a large house; they simply build up the nest by stacking the twigs until it is the right height. They seem to use any hole size, from 1⅛" to 1½" (2.9cm to 3.8cm) or even larger, no matter what the bird books say. (I've found that birds don't read the bird books, they only want to build nests.) We can help them by making birdhouses that are as safe as possible for them. The ever-popular bluebirds will be attracted to this house, as well as the amiable indigo bunting and white tree swallow. Chickadees, wrens, titmice and nuthatches will also gladly make it their home.

This house is similar to the Acorn Wren House, but it is a little larger and has another window, another step and Y-shaped roof supports instead of a single branch. Cedar, aspen, cottonwood, birch, pine, ash or other soft woods can be used. I used mountain ash. The log should be about 7" to 8" (17.8cm to 18.3cm) in diameter and 10" (25.4cm) tall before the roof angles are cut. You may have to make this house a little shorter to fit in your band saw if you do not have an extension for it (see page 12 of the "Getting Started" section). If you want to make a medium-size songbird house and do not have a band saw, you can use a 6" (15.2cm) plastic pipe or an oatmeal box. The project house is made to hang from a hook or tree, but if you prefer a pole mount, simply omit the rope.

## MATERIALS

house body: a log that is 7" (17.8cm) in diameter and 10" (25.4cm) tall • ¼" (6.4mm) exterior plywood for floor • two roof pieces about 8½" (21.6cm) square (I used roof shakes) • roof ridge about 10" (25.4cm) long and 4½" (11.4cm) in diameter • roof ridge support • limb for chimney about 1" (2.5cm) in diameter and 2½"(6.4cm) long • two Eyebrows, one to fit over the door hole and a smaller one to go over the lower window • pair of large Ys for the roof supports • pair of small Ys for the roof supports • one small Y for the porch support • one half-round wood slice for the porch • three smaller half-round slices for the steps and the window shelf • three seedpods (eucalyptus were used here) for the step and shelf support • twigs for the windows crosspieces • no. 8 screw eye • 2' (61cm) of sisal rope • acrylic paint

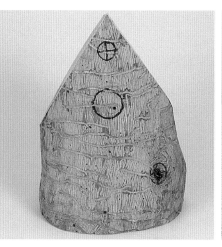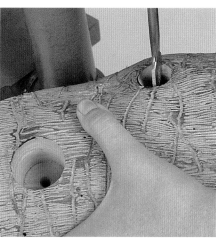

**1** Draw the design on the log.
Draw your house design on the log, allowing enough distance between elements so it doesn't look crowded. The center of the bird hole is about 5½" (14cm) above the floor and the lower edge of the window is about 1" (2.5cm) above that. The edge of the lower window is 2" (5.1cm) above the floor and 2" (5.1cm) from the vertical center line. The door hole size is 1⅜" (3.5cm) and the windows are ¾" (1.9cm), although ⅞" (2.2cm) is fine.

**2** Cut the roof angles.
Once you are happy with the design, cut the roof angles as described on page 18.

**3** Drill the bird and window holes.
Next, drill the bird and window holes with the appropriate spade bit and an electric drill or drill press.

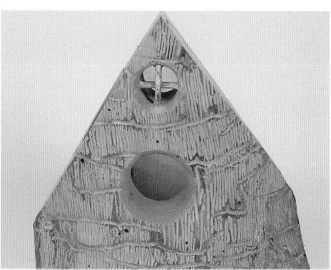

**5** Rasp and paint the hole edges.
Now it's time to rasp and paint the window and doorway openings. When the paint is dry, add the window twigs as described on page 26.

**4** Core the house.
Core the house as explained on page 19. Then glue and nail the house back together, making sure that the front and the back are flush and the bottoms are even. Try to get all the glue off the outer surface of the house before it sets, and fill any gaps with sawdust as described on page 15.

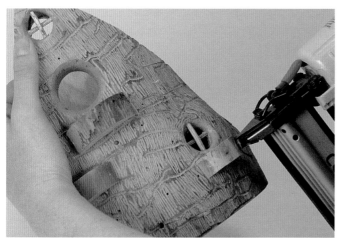

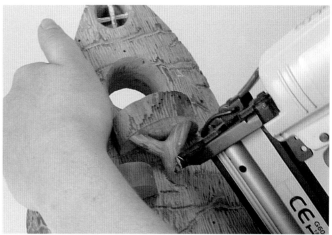

**6** Add the porch and steps.
The pieces for the porch and steps are sliced from two sizes of limbs—one slightly larger than the bird hole for the porch piece, and three smaller ones that are a little larger than the window hole. The slices are about ¾" (1.9cm) thick and curved to fit the front of the log. The steps are spaced about the same distance apart as the thickness of the steps and are on the side opposite the window. When placing the steps, leave room for a support under the porch. Also, you will be placing your Ys under the eaves of the roof, so you do not want to put the steps too far to the side. Hold the supports up to the house to be sure there's room for them. When you are happy with the placement of the porch, steps and window shelf, glue and nail them.

**7** Rasp, sand and attach the Y.
Before you attach the small Y under the porch, shape it to fit by rasping it and sanding it. Then glue and nail it in place.

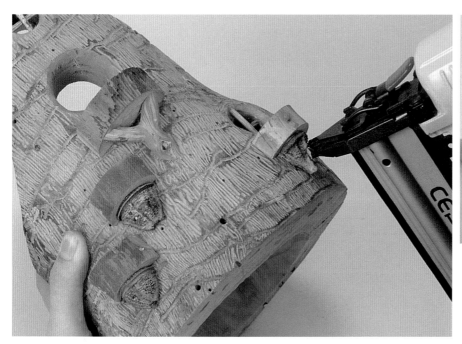

**9** Add the Eyebrows.
Next, shape the Eyebrows to fit over the door and the lower window. Glue and nail them in place.

**8** Add seedpods.
Cut to fit, and attach the three seedpods under the two steps and the window. Eucalyptus seedpods are nice to work with because they smell wonderful when they are cut in half and sanded.

**10** Add the floor, roof, roof ridge and support.

Add the roof, the roof ridge, the roof ridge support and the floor as described on pages 20–25. Remember that if this house is really for the birds, attach the floor with screws instead of glue and nails so that it can be cleaned out.

**11** Add the Ys.

Start sanding the lower and upper Ys as shown on pages 27–28, so that the angles fit. The lower ones are placed at the lower line of the porch and the upper ones fit in the area between the upper window and the door hole. Shaping these pieces to fit may take some practice and patience. I make my lower Ys from branches that are about index finger-size. However, chubbier ones or thinner ones also look fine—it depends on your taste and on what you can readily find. After the Ys are sanded to fit, glue and nail them in place.

**12** Add the chimney.

The final steps are adding the chimney, which is described on page 30, and attaching a rope the same way as on the Acorn Wren House, page 106.

You now have the friendliest bird home you could ever care to make, and the birds will love you for it.

**This house** is made from an aspen log and shows how nicely a flair at the base of the wood can be used to set off the design. The light color is also attractive. The houses can either be mounted on a post in the garden or hung from a porch or a tree. They should be at least 5' (1.5m) off the ground. A hanging house is somewhat more secure than a post in regards to cats and other predators.

**This house** is made from the same type of wood as the project house (mountain ash). It shows the variation in texture and color that is always present in nature—no two houses are ever alike. The little welcome sign over the door is cut from a soft wood, painted with acrylics and varnished to help preserve it.

# Bluebird Wall House

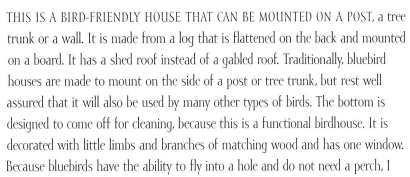

THIS IS A BIRD-FRIENDLY HOUSE THAT CAN BE MOUNTED ON A POST, a tree trunk or a wall. It is made from a log that is flattened on the back and mounted on a board. It has a shed roof instead of a gabled roof. Traditionally, bluebird houses are made to mount on the side of a post or tree trunk, but rest well assured that it will also be used by many other types of birds. The bottom is designed to come off for cleaning, because this is a functional birdhouse. It is decorated with little limbs and branches of matching wood and has one window. Because bluebirds have the ability to fly into a hole and do not need a perch, I have replaced the porch with a decorative branch. My observation is that the birds can perch on the edge of the hole if they want. If you have several trees in your yard, you may want to make several of these houses to see all the kinds of birds this design will attract. The house should be mounted 4' to 6' (1.2m to 1.8m) above the ground. Bluebirds like to make their homes in open fields, with water and trees nearby.

The project house is made from a birch log, but I've also used cedar firewood logs. Since the back of the log will be cut flat, this is a good opportunity to use an imperfect log that's unsuitable for other projects. The decorative touches on the house are cut from aspen and painted to look like birch. This house goes together pretty quickly and you may want to try different variations once you have made a few.

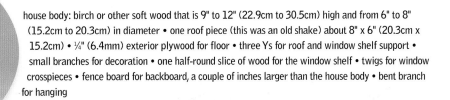

MATERIALS

house body: birch or other soft wood that is 9" to 12" (22.9cm to 30.5cm) high and from 6" to 8" (15.2cm to 20.3cm) in diameter • one roof piece (this was an old shake) about 8" x 6" (20.3cm x 15.2cm) • ¼" (6.4mm) exterior plywood for floor • three Ys for roof and window shelf support • small branches for decoration • one half-round slice of wood for the window shelf • twigs for window crosspieces • fence board for backboard, a couple of inches larger than the house body • bent branch for hanging

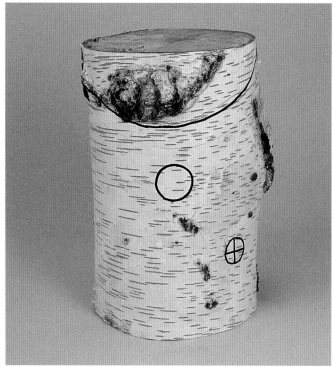

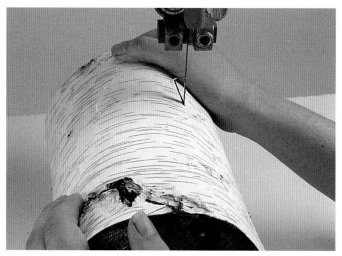

## 2 Cut the log.

Use the band saw to cut a slice off the back of the log about two-thirds of the way back, allowing for a nesting cavity about 4" (10.2cm) deep. This cut needs to be as straight as possible so the house can be mounted on the board. Of course you can even it up with a rasp or by sanding it after coring.

## 1 Draw the design on your log.

Draw your design on your log. The size of the bird hole is 1⅜". (3.5cm) and is centered on the front about 5" (12.7cm) from the floor. (This hole should be placed higher if you have a taller log.) The window hole is ⅞" (2.2cm) and is 2" to 3" (5.1cm to x7.6cm) from the floor and set off to the right. The slope of the shed roof is gentle, dropping about 1" (2.5cm) from the back cut.

## 3 Cut the roof angles.

The next cut is the roof cut. Again, try to cut even and straight. Once the house is cored, it is quite easy to go back and even this up, if necessary. On the other hand, I've found that houses that are not cut perfectly straight have a great sense of character and often are more charming than the ones cut perfectly straight.

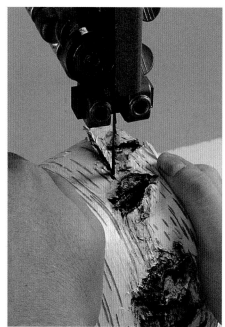

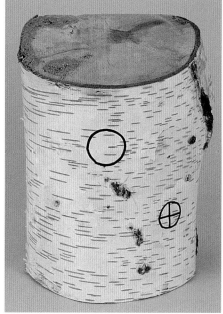

*This is how the house will look with its sloped roof and flat back.*

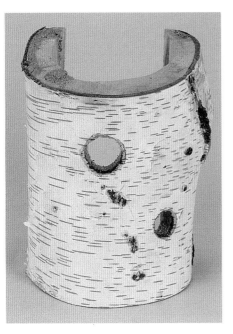

**4** Drill the holes and core the house.
Drill the window and bird holes as explained on page 18, then core the house body as shown on page 19. Of course, this house will have only one half to core instead of two. After coring, trace the bottom of the house onto the plywood and cut out the floor.

**5** Glue the house body on the backboard.
Next, line up the house on the backboard. I always eyeball this placement, but you can mark it with a pencil if you like. The house is fairly centered on the board, with a little more room on the bottom. Use hot glue to mount the house on the backboard.

**7** Insert the screws in backboard and floor.
Next, turn the house around, drill pilot holes and set the screws into the sidewalls of the house from the back. You can make sure you are getting the screws into the wall by looking from the top down into the house. Place two screws on each side. Always keep in mind not to get too close to any edge so that the screws will not split the wood.

Next, attach the floor of the house with screws. Paint the front edge to blend it in with the backboard.

**6** Apply pressure.
Hold the house in place for a minute or so, applying some pressure until the glue sets.

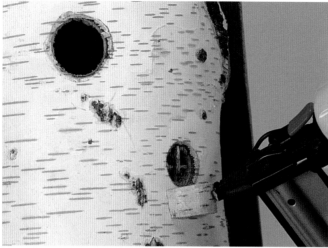

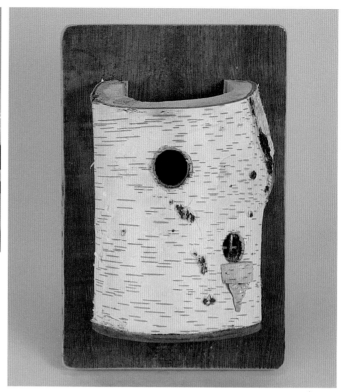

## 8 Decorate the window.

Now rasp the bird hole and the window. Set in the twigs for the window as you have done before (or use wire for durability). Add the window shelf and the little branch support under the shelf, fitting the pieces first by rasping or sanding. This is covered in detail on pages 73–74. A seedpod can be substituted as a shelf support.

## 9 Make the roof.

Cut a roof piece with about a 1" (2.5cm) overhang. Round the corners to match the shape of the log and bevel the back edge to match the slope of the roof. This can be done easily with a rasp or sanding block. Glue the roof with Titebond II or Elmer's Squeeze'n Caulk, then add screws. If the roof does not lie flat because the shake is warped, slowly tightening the screws will often flatten it. Do this carefully to avoid cracking the wood. If it cracks, refer to the glue-and-sawdust technique described on page 15.

## 10 Add the decorative branch.

Now it's time to add the decorative branch to the front of the house. Move it around until you find a pleasing position. Then sand the back of it, glue it and nail it with brads.

## 11 Add the final decorative touches.

I added a little piece over the window and some small Ys under the roof overhang to complete the house.

*After you have cut and sanded the decorative branches to fit, you'll want to paint them to match the house if your house is made from birch. Paint a basecoat of ivory acrylic paint, then add brown lines with a small pointed brush to look like birch bark. Just follow the piece of birch wood to determine the color and the pattern of lines.*

## 12 Add a hanger.

The last step is to add the elbow-shaped branch that serves as a hanger at the top of the backboard. This needs to be a strong piece of wood and must be glued with a strong glue such as Titebond II, and nailed with two or three nails on each side. When I hang this house outdoors, I hang it on a stout nail or screw. Next, I drill two holes in the sides of the backboard for long screws that go into the post or wall. This will keep the house from being knocked down by the wind, a cat or anything else.

# Hollow Log House

THIS HOUSE IS SPECIAL because it is made from a found hollow log. A naturally hollow log is not easy to find, but when one comes your way, you must seize the opportunity! Finding such a log was the event that first inspired me to make a house from a tree. I had been working with twigs and branches as decoration on square houses and I was in the woods collecting them when I spotted a hollow log. It occurred to me that I could easily make a round house by cutting the log to size and adding a roof and floor. That first house was quite a success; when I wanted to make more, I devised my coring technique as a way of making the hollow log myself. As it turned out, everyone from the UPS man to the grocer found out I made houses from hollow logs and started collecting them for me. So if you wish to make this project and you can't find a suitable log, I suggest you put the word out among your friends and see what comes your way.

In the woods, these trees provide homes for many small creatures and birds and are fondly referred to as critter trees. I always tell people to thoroughly inspect any hollow tree they discover and make sure no creature is living in it before they take it.

Large houses look nice when mounted on a post, so this house was designed that way. It has a porch roof like the Mountain Gnome Home. There are three windows, two of which have roofs. It has two sets of Ys like the Woodland Songbird House, and there is an acorn light by the bird hole. The symmetry of this design suits a house that is a little broader in shape than the other houses. The assembly of all the parts is the same as the Woodland Songbird House. Since you do not have to core this house, it will go together quickly. Have fun with this special find.

## MATERIALS

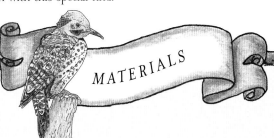

house body: hollow log, about 10" (25.4cm) tall • ¼" (6.4mm) exterior plywood for floor • two roof pieces about 9" (22.9cm) square (these are made from old shakes) • three smaller roof pieces for the porch and window roofs • branch about 10½" (26.7cm) long and 6" (15.2cm) in diameter for the roof ridge • roof ridge support • two small branch pieces for porch roof support • branch for the chimney, 1" (2.5cm) in diameter and 2½" (6.4cm) long • pair of large Ys for the lower roof supports • pair of small Ys for the upper roof supports • three small Ys for porch and window shelf supports • three half-round limb slices for porch and window shelves • acorn for door light • twigs for six window crosspieces • acrylic paints

This house will be made of whatever kind of wood you happen to find that is hollow. Sometimes a hollow log might be so decayed that it's cracked or unstable. Often you can still salvage it by impregnating the weak parts with a good wood glue. This technique is covered on page 15. Your log should be at least 6" (15.2cm) in diameter, but it can be quite a bit larger. If it happens to be smaller than this, you can make it into a fairy or gnome home, since it will be too small for a functional birdhouse. Of course, you can go ahead and make it into a really small birdhouse to use for decoration. For all the decorative details, choose branches with colors that complement the color of your log.

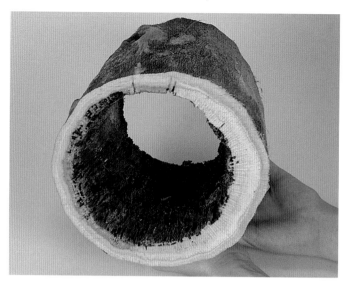

Inspect your hollow log before using it to build a house. The outer walls should be nice and firm with the inside completely decayed and gone. Starting with a hollow log simplifies the process since you will not have to core it.

## 1 Draw the design on your log.

Draw the design of the house on the log. This log was cut to 10" (25.4cm) tall, and it is 8" (20.3cm) in diameter. The center of the bird hole is about 5" (12.7cm) from the bottom, and the center of the window is 2¼" (5.7cm) above that. The centers of the lower windows are about 2½" (6.4cm) from the bottom and 5" (12.7cm) apart from center to center. The symmetry of this house is pleasing with the lower windows at the same level and distance from the center.

## 2 Cut the roof angles.

Now cut the roof angles as described on page 18.

## 3 Drill the holes.

Drill the holes for the bird hole and windows. The bird hole is 1⅜" (3.5mm) and the windows are ⅞" (2.2mm). Because the house is already hollow, there will be a greater risk of the wood splitting when you drill it. The key is to have a sharp drill bit and to go slowly and steadily, avoiding vibration as you drill. If the wood does split, don't give up. Glue it well and use a couple of rubber bands to hold it until the glue dries.

## 4 Add the window crosspieces and floor.

Rasp the holes and paint them. Then add the twigs in the windows as shown on page 26. Next, make and attach the floor as described on pages 20–21.

## 5 Add the roof, roof ridge, ridge support and chimney.

Then add the roof, with its ridge and support, and the chimney. All these steps are covered in detail on pages 22–25 and page 30.

## 6 Add the window shelves and porches.

The window shelves and porches are half-round pieces of limbs. Rasp the straight side into a moon shape so they will fit the curve of the house. Glue and nail the shelves and porches in place. Then glue and nail the Ys underneath them.

### 7 Add the Ys.

Now add your two sets of Ys, leaving room for the piece that will go over the porch. It's best to cut that piece now and hold it in place before gluing and nailing the Ys. If the fit is too tight, you can rasp or sand the pieces before you attach them to the house.

### 8 Add the porch and window roofs.

The last steps are to add the little roofs over the bird hole and windows. This technique is shown on page 79 of the Mountain Gnome Home. As a final touch, you can add the acorn by the bird hole as shown on page 66. Your hollow log house is now ready for occupancy.

**This** *was a little hollow aspen log that just happened to have a natural hole in it, making a perfect door opening. Such finds are both exciting and rare. Watching for them is like a wonderful treasure hunt, and finding them is cause for great rejoicing. It makes me think of the old adage, "the best things in life are free."*

# Gallery

**Top left:** *This large songbird house shows the use of a nice bulge made into a window and the addition of a door below the bird hole.*

**Middle right:** *This house is called a Fairy Apartment as it has several rooms to it. There is also a wren house built into the second story. This shows how creative you can be once you get the idea of coring out logs and limbs. This house was about 2' (61cm) tall, but was made manageable by cutting it into sections and then gluing and nailing it back together again.*

**Bottom left:** *This two-room house is called a Mountain Lodge. It is not difficult to add a room onto the side of a gnome home or a fairy house once you become familiar with the techniques. A nice, natural hole provided a perfect door, and a scar in one of the smaller logs provided a closed door such as that in the Gnome-Is-Not-Home project.*

# Index

# Get Creative
## with North Light Books!

### Create Your Own Tabletop Fountains

You can create your own tabletop fountains and add beautiful accents to your living room, bedroom, kitchen and garden. These fifteen gorgeous step-by-step projects make it easy, using everything from lava rock and bamboo, to shells and clay pots. You'll learn to incorporate flowers, driftwood, fire, figurines, crystals, plants and more to create works of art that will have friends buzzing for years to come.

1-58180-103-3, paperback, 128 pages, #31791-K

### Creative Wedding Florals You Can Make

Create your very own floral arrangements for priceless wedding memories with a personal touch. Terry Rye, a professional florist with twenty years of experience, will show you how to design more than twenty stunning floral arrangements. You'll find something for every part of your wedding—from the bride's bouquet to boutonnieres, from pew decorations to table centerpieces and wedding cake toppers.

1-55870-560-0, paperback, 128 pages, #70488-K

### Creating Life-Like Animals in Polymer Clay

With the easy-to-use medium of polymer clay and this extraordinary book, you can learn to create exquisitely detailed animal sculptures that are full of personality. Inside you'll find step-by-step instructions for ten charming projects, including bluebirds, white-tailed fawns, basset hounds, rabbits, bears and more. You'll even learn how to model animals to look like bronze or jade.

0-89134-955-3, paperback, 128 pages, #31428-K

### Gourd Fun For Everyone

Create incredible characters with gourds! Sammie Crawford, The Fairy Gourdmother, shows you how, with painting techniques, decorating ideas, patterns and practical instructions. Eight step-by-step projects, including a frog prince, a snowman, a lighthouse, and a bow-legged cowboy, make it easy and fun. Additional examples will inspire your own ideas of what a gourd can be.

0-89134-993-6, paperback, 128 pages, #31544-K

**These books and other fine North Light titles are available from your local art & craft retailer, bookstore, online supplier or by calling (800) 221-5831.**